SPECIAL PLACES;
SPECIAL PEOPLE

The hidden curriculum of school grounds

WWF

CW00448998

Wendy Titman
Learning through Landscapes

Published by WWF UK (World Wide Fund For Nature),
Panda House, Weyside Park, Godalming, Surrey GU7 1XR, UK.

A catalogue record for this book is available from The British Library.

ISBN: 0 947613 48 X

This book is printed on paper which is from renewable timber, produced on a fully sustainable basis.
The pulp used in the manufacture of this paper is bleached without the use of
chlorine gas (Elemental Chlorine Free)

Designed by: Howland ■ Northover, Cranleigh.
Printed by: Rayment Printers, Dorking.

Contents

Preface

Special Places; Special People is the result of two years of collaboration between WWF, an international environmental organisation, and Learning through Landscapes, the UK charity concerned with all aspects of school grounds. It focuses on a critical period in everyone's lives - the formative experiences of the school yard.

When we embarked on this research we both had a strong belief that there were powerful connections between school grounds and children's views of the environment and the adults who spoil or cherish it. *Special Places; Special People* has provided the qualitative evidence that this is indeed the case.

It is comparatively rare that children are asked directly about what they think or feel but we were keen to do just that. While it is, of course, the job of the headteacher to manage a school, we believe it to be important to listen carefully to the voices of young people.

As the world becomes a more dangerous place and children's freedom to roam decreases, so the school grounds, as a safe open space, becomes ever more important - a special place for generations of special people.

Bill Lucas,
Director of Learning through Landscapes

Peter Martin,
Principal Education Officer, WWF UK

ABOUT WWF

WWF is an international environmental organisation with national groups around the world. Launched in 1961, WWF has supported over 5,000 projects in 130 countries, and has invested over £230 million in conservation over the last 10 years.

WWF UK is committed to a broadly based environmental education programme. As part of this programme, resource materials are produced which aim to enable teachers to bring environmental issues into everyday classroom teaching, and to give young people the knowledge and experience they need in order to make informed personal judgements about these issues.

Resources are being developed for subjects across the entire school curriculum, making use of the inherent qualities of each subject to develop specific aspects of environmental understanding and sensitivity. In addition, WWF has in progress projects designed to help teachers plan, implement and evaluate effective cross-curricular environmental education.

'Reaching Out', WWF's INSET programme for both Primary and Secondary teachers, is now available on a regional basis across the UK. Also in development are a number of innovative electronic data delivery projects which will give schools, colleges and individuals access to WWF's expertise, data, reports and fact sheets.

In addition to courses and resources, WWF runs a free Teacher Representative Scheme for all schools. Registered schools receive WWF's termly teachers' newsletter, *Lifelines*, details of all new resources, plus a discount on all education materials.

If you would like further details about WWF's education programme, please write to: WWF UK, Education, Panda House, Weyside Park, Godalming, Surrey GU7 1XR, or telephone: 0483 426444.

ABOUT LEARNING THROUGH LANDSCAPES

Learning through Landscapes (LTL) was launched in 1990 as an independent charity. It is the only national organisation concerned solely with all aspects of school grounds.

LTL provides an extensive range of publications and videos. It also has an extensive data-base on which thousands of school grounds schemes are listed.

LTL runs a number of sponsored projects with Esso, BT, British Rail, Marks & Spencer and the Post Office. Each of these aim to enliven and improve some aspect of grounds development.

LTL places particularly high value on research and training and we are continually developing new initiatives in these areas.

As a membership organisation we are always keen to encourage new supporters. If you would like more information about any aspect of our work, please contact: Learning through Landscapes, 3rd Floor, Southside Offices, The Law Courts, Winchester, Hampshire SO23 9DL.

Introduction

This document is the culmination of a research project entitled 'Special Places; Special People' which began in 1990 and took almost three years to complete.

One of the primary aims of the project was that it should ultimately assist those involved in the management of schools and their grounds for the benefit of children.

To that end this document is presented as a working manual rather than simply a research report. It is divided into four sections. Section One provides background information about the project and a short review of existing research; Section Two presents selected material gathered during our own research, together with a summary of our Findings; Section Three contains a discusson of key issues arising from the research which we believe have major implications for all schools, together with some suggested ways of approaching the process of change; Section Four provides an alphabetical listing of references, together with a selection of additional useful material.

The intention in using this format is to facilitate consideration of the research within the context of some of the 'real life' pressures, constraints and opportunities with which those who manage schools today are commonly faced. We therefore hope that this document will not only inform and enthuse but also encourage and enable change.

Acknowledgements

This research project would not have been possible without the support, help and co-operation of a great many adults and children. All of the interviews with children were held in schools. However, because the research was concerned to identify children's responses to types of environments and elements of them rather than to investigate specific locations, the schools which assisted with the project have not been identified. In addition, the children who agreed to take part were assured that their comments would not be attributed to them personally. All the unascribed quotations which appear in the margins of this document are taken from transcripts of these interviews.

However, as those who gave of their time know who they are, I trust that they will accept our grateful thanks and gain some satisfaction from realising how invaluable their contribution has been to this work.

The development of the methodology which formed the basis of the research project relied upon the considerable expertise of Virginia Valentine of Semiotic Solutions. My gratitude to Ginny extends well beyond this fact. Her deep commitment to the aims of the project coupled with her endless generosity in sharing, explaining and exploring the complexities of semiotics is surely the trademark of true professionalism.

I also wish to record my thanks to Peter Martin (WWF UK) and Bill Lucas (LTL), not only for commissioning this study in the first place, but especially for their faith and commitment to genuinely open-ended research.

I am also grateful to those within both agencies who helped with the research and the production of this document, particularly Kirsty Young for her patience in helping me grapple with the wonders of computer technology, and Joan Wood for her continual willingness to listen, consider and advise. Thanks are also due for the use of LTL's photographs which I have used to illustrate this document, along with my own.

Whilst the research is presented in this document as one overall project, it will become clear to the reader that it actually involved a number of separate but inter-related elements which received support and assistance from a variety of sources. One of these elements involved research into the effect of introducing small equipment into school grounds at playtime. We are grateful to Mike Sleap and his staff from Hull University School of Education for undertaking this research on our behalf, to the schools which participated and to NES Arnold for supplying the equipment. We are grateful to David Gent, Managing Director of Lappsett UK for financial support to the project overall.

In *Children's Experience of Place*, Roger Hart explores the significance of personal childhood experiences in terms of his research. As a result of undertaking this study I have no doubt that the process of immersing oneself in child-centred research of this kind inevitably provokes such reflection. For me, the experience engendered a renewed appreciation of my own good fortune in having had a childhood filled with a sense of wonder about the world around me and for the opportunity to explore it. For this lasting legacy I pay tribute to my parents.

Finally, I thank my husband Gordon for being so supportive, tolerant and indulgent!

Having completed the research I took advantage of the goodwill of a number of friends and colleagues in seeking advice about the most appropriate format for this document. I would like to record my gratitude to Steve Ball, Head of Edwalton School; Alan Marshall, Head of Bevois Town School; Zoe Rydderch- Evans, Head of Cowick First School, and Katie Samuels, Head of St. Jude's School, for giving their time and advice so generously and for their collective wisdom in suggesting "let the children say it".

As a result, the last word must surely go to a small person who, whilst accompanying me on an 'expedition' around his school grounds, enquired demandingly, "But why are you doing it - this research stuff? Will it make any difference, else what's the point?"... I ask you.

Wendy Titman

vi

SECTION ONE
Background to the project

This Section contains:

◆ An explanation of the research project and its objectives.

◆ A review of existing research which considers:
- The use of school grounds within educational tradition
- The significance of environmental experience in childhood
- The relationship between place-identity and self-identity
- The influence of culture on children's use of external environments
- Play and the external environment
- Children's views and preferences in terms of external environments.

◆ Details of the research brief including an explanation of the semiotic approach, methodology and an example of one of the collage boards used.

◆ References.

1 Background to the research project

1.1 INTRODUCTION

As with all good research, it is often the case that more questions exist at the end than had at the beginning! The first phase of the Learning through Landscapes (LTL) project was remarkably successful and extremely influential. The *Final Report* written by Eileen Adams[1] is testament to the breadth, depth and far-sightedness of the work undertaken during that time. Despite this fact, or maybe because of it, by the time the report was completed a further list of questions had arisen which required equally vigorous investigation.

The fact that stereotypical school grounds are a wasted resource had long been recognised. LTL's initial research phase gathered ample evidence identifying the benefits of development of school grounds for use as 'outdoor classrooms'. Furthermore, certain types of changes in the physical design of the grounds and the way they were managed, were shown to have resulted in improvement in the Informal Curriculum in terms of children's attitude and behaviour during play and playtime. However, it had not been possible to investigate the causes of the changes in sufficient detail at that stage.

Many of those who had embarked upon the development of school grounds were convinced that in addition to the benefits of specific changes, other less tangible benefits accrued as a result of the process of change which had a significant impact on the operation of their school as a whole.

Examples cited include a reduction in vandalism; changes in social behaviour and attitude; the development of a new ethos of care for the place and the people in it; increased levels of community interest and involvement; a reduction in truancy levels; improvements in discipline, and generally that "everyone somehow seems happier – even the school keeper"!

1

The *Final Report* from the initial research phase highlights the fact that many of these benefits relate to what it identified as the 'Hidden Curriculum' of school grounds. However, the strength of evidence indicated that further research was required in order to attempt to distinguish between the causes and effects of what is often a complex process, involving both physical and managerial changes and the impact these can have on the attitudes and feelings of all those involved.

When LTL was launched as a trust in 1990, these issues framed the basis of a further study which was subsequently funded by WWF UK (World Wide Fund For Nature). The two year research project came to be known as *'Special Places: Special People'*.

1.2 THE OBJECTIVES OF 'SPECIAL PLACES: SPECIAL PEOPLE'

Essentially the research was driven by one over-arching question: does the physical environment of school grounds and the way they are managed affect children's attitude/behaviour, and if so how/why? Within this broad question there were many elements: for example, How does the environment affect and influence children? Do certain types of places produce consistent responses from them? What factors influence these responses? What sorts of places do children value and why?

From the above, four key areas were identified for investigation:

i) The significance of the Hidden Curriculum of school grounds.

ii) The relationship between the management of the Informal Curriculum and children's attitude/behaviour.

iii) The correlation, if any, between the design of the environment of school grounds and the quality of children's experience.

iv) The critical elements in the process of change and development of school grounds in terms of children's attitude and behaviour.

2 Brief summary of existing research review

The first task was to identify and, if possible, examine existing research covering the elements identified for investigation. This had a dual function in that it created a data base of valuable information but it also ensured that, in determining the need for new research, we would hopefully avoid re-creating wheels!

Initially, very little research material was found which related specifically to children's use of school grounds. However, when the exercise was broadened to include the impact of the physical environment in general on children's attitude and behaviour a great deal of valuable material was found. It is significant to note here that our investigations led us to explore a diverse range of fields including environmental, ecological and behavioural psychology, anthropology, philosophy, geography, architecture, planning, leisure and, of course, education.

Most revealing of all was the fact that whilst much of this research *concerned* children, relatively little material could be found which actually *involved* children. This point clearly merited careful consideration. Many researchers cite the difficulty of obtaining reliable data from children as a reason for not involving them in the research process. Yet others, for whom children's views and opinions were fundamental, created methodologies designed to enable this objective thereby producing a rich source of data as well as an interesting range of research models.

The database continued to expand as the research project progressed, but this initial phase was invaluable in informing the study and helping to refine both our fields of enquiry and methodology.

The huge scope of material involved in the review of research defies even scant record here, but it is useful to highlight some of the key subject areas which had particular bearing on the project and some of the material which proved particularly helpful.

2.1 THE USE OF SCHOOL GROUNDS WITHIN EDUCATIONAL TRADITION

Whilst the creation of LTL in the mid eighties was undoubtedly a landmark, many of the concepts which it advocates are not new. In addition to providing for physical education, sport and games, evidence exists of schools using their grounds for a wide range of teaching and learning opportunities before the turn of the century, and certainly the practice was not uncommon before the last World War.

In her fascinating book *Time to Play in Early Childhood Education*[2], Tina Bruce examines the philosophies of some of the most influential early educationalists and includes many references to the emphasis placed on the use of school grounds as an integral part of education.

The extent to which school grounds were, historically, valued as an essential resource for all aspects of the curriculum is apparent from works such as *Child Life in Our Schools* published in 1906[3]. In this Mabel Brown produces a detailed timetable showing how the 'garden and sand beach' in her school were used throughout the year for all aspects of the curriculum including geography which was then a new subject! Miss Brown also testifies to the fact that children were just as enthusiastic about having a garden in those days as they are today.

In addition to exhorting the better use of school grounds for a wide range of educational purposes, evidence exists that some education-alists have long recognised the need to campaign and lobby to extend and develop school grounds. Thus, Miss E.R. Boyce (described as a 'Sometime Assistant Inspector of Education') in a book first published in 1939[4] bemoans the fact that "whilst many schools have a garden, the Headmaster often thinks that the small children in the Infants' Department cannot keep a garden". She advocates that this is so valuable an exercise for them that the Infants' teacher should "beg a small piece for their exclusive use".

"It is interesting to note that for Froebel, McMillan and Isaacs, it was the child's free play in the garden which led to their greatest contributions to the early childhood educational curriculum." Bruce[2]

"Every interval finds the children round the garden, their little noses and hands pressed against the trellis work and alas! to tell the truth - their little feet also. I frequently have to be humbly and deeply apologetic to the surveyor for those 'unaccountable' holes. Unfortunately he sometimes gives my children's pardonable curiosity and interest another name." Brown[3]

Brief summary of existing research review

It is often assumed that such provision was the norm for Infants, yet according to Miss Boyce it was more common for such provision to be made for junior age children. With true missionary zeal Miss Boyce goes on to suggest that teachers should also seek to acquire any piece of waste ground close to the school: "Many authorities have agreed to dig up asphalt to provide gardens for small children. They might, if asked, do the same to provide a piece of waste ground."

By the late 1960s, the "uniformly dismal green deserts" that constituted many school grounds prompted Eric Hart and Alan Shaw, (Lancashire County Council Architects Department) and Ian Laurie (University of Manchester School of Landscape Architecture) to produce a research brief to look into all aspects of site planning and design in order to make proposals for better use of school land. The research project resulted in a comprehensive handbook being produced in 1977, though no evidence of it being published could be found. The *School Site Planning Handbook* [5] deals substantially with design and technical aspects of school grounds, and there is heavy emphasis on use for physical education though other aspects are included.

A further element of this research project involved consultation with children and a document entitled *Ask the Kids* [6] was subsequently published containing children's views and opinions about school grounds. This is described in more detail later in this section.

From this element of the research review it appears that it was once quite commonplace for schools to utilise the land around their buildings for many aspects of the formal as well as the informal curriculum. However, the tradition waned during the past three decades or so to the point that, in the main, school grounds became used only for PE, games and 'playtime', with the exception of a few remarkable pioneers who continued to recognise and utilise this valuable resource for a wide range of educational purposes.

"In the waste ground the children will trench, dig, make rivers, hills and valleys, pools and streams. They may try to float boats, bury hidden treasure and make see-saws of planks and logs. They will find caterpillars and worms, ants and slugs, and stop what they are doing to examine them. Waste ground, with trees and rubbish and perhaps a ditch, is the best plaything a child can be given. Geography is easily learned and wild fantasies worked out in the health-giving open air."
Boyce [4]

2.2 THE SIGNIFICANCE OF ENVIRONMENTAL EXPERIENCE IN CHILDHOOD

For many, perhaps the majority of adults, some of their strongest memories and recollections of childhood relate to places, often 'outdoor' places. Feelings are engendered by memories of particular places, and places evoke certain 'feeling responses'. Whilst it was never our intention to embark upon a study of individual, psychological responses to the environment, we were concerned to understand whether, to any extent, certain types of environments produce given responses in children. We also wanted to discover whether there were any common factors which influenced environmental experience other than on an individual and personal level.

One of the first major studies of the impact of environmental experience in childhood was conducted by Edith Cobb[7] who reviewed 300 autobiographical recollections of childhood of famous people. From this Cobb claimed a correlation between the development of creativity and ecological experience in childhood.

In order to test Cobb's findings, Louise Chawla[8] replicated the study in 1986 using a smaller number of different autobiographies including people from a more diverse social and professional spectrum. Chawla questions the universality of Cobb's findings, but in so doing Chawla finds some remarkably unambiguous associations and concludes that certain types of memory occurred under certain conditions with "lawful regularity".

Chawla defines seven forms of environmental memory which she describes as:
◆ Transcendence
◆ Affection
◆ Ambivalence
◆ Idealization
◆ Rejection
◆ Detachment
◆ Omission.

Memories of exciting places predominated in her research, characterised by intense rather than repetitive experience. Furthermore, she finds that outdoor places were remembered out of all proportion to the relative number of hours spent there.

In relation to transcendence, Chawla notes that freedom and a natural environment were almost invariable factors and that the opportunity to consider the environment one's own, to touch and explore without fear of transgression, was essential.

Affection was always associated with places that were valued by the adults around the child as well as by the child itself, and involved exploration and discovery in places that children appropriated as their own. Chawla explains the difference between affection and transcendence as involving the "social embeddedness of the place".

In summary, Chawla finds that physical factors alone were insufficient as determinants of environmental memory because social, cultural and personal factors were equally significant and that a key element for children relates to the extent to which places engender a sense of belonging. This work suggests that the 'semiotics' of places, the messages and meanings which are conveyed, are very influential in terms of the significance of environmental experience in childhood.

2.3   THE RELATIONSHIP BETWEEN PLACE-IDENTITY AND SELF-IDENTITY

The relationship between place-identity and self-identity is a subject which, from our review of research, holds considerable significance in terms of children's environmental experience. Chawla draws attention to the work of Relph in her study in examining the development of a sense of ownership and belonging. It is important to note that the concept of ownership as it is used here is not necessarily literal, more that the messages and meanings conveyed by the place enable it to be claimed as 'mine' or 'ours' rather than being, in any sense, 'theirs'.

Transcendence is explained as "memory of a dynamic relationship with the outer world, of a profound continuity with natural processes involving elation, sense of exuberance, or enveloping calm, of timelessness, boundlessness and radiance".

Affection is described as "memory of places to which we trace our roots, which are associated with happiness and security. It incorporates social definitions of the environment and there is a parallel between the warmth of feeling for the place and the people in it".

Ambivalence "results when the dominant culture devalues this place. It cannot be rejected because it is where one's personality and perspective developed and there are therefore ties of affection but neither can it be comfortably embraced".

Rejection "occurs when the environment represents a place to escape from, because of what it is or isn't in reality or in terms of it's meanings and symbols". Chawla[8]

"The forms of environment which people in (her) study cherished, which were integral to their self identity, conform to the concept of existential insideness which Relph (1976) defined as a sense of belonging to a place, a sense of knowing that this place is where one belongs, a feeling of being part of a place and of it's being part of oneself". Chawla[8]

"To be attached to places and have profound ties with them is an important human need." Relph[9]

Relph in *Place and Placelessness*[9] explains existential insideness as "the inner structure of space as it appears to us in our concrete experience of the world as members of a cultural group". In other words we form judgements about places; who they are for or belong to; whether they can be 'owned'; whether they are places 'for me' or 'people like me', and what we can do in and with them. This is because, as individuals within the cultural structure of society, we understand a common set of signs and symbols or 'signifiers' which we both read from, and into, places. As Relph explains it, places are therefore understood "as centres of meaning or focuses of intention and purpose".

"Spaces and places must necessarily be fundamental considerations in (the) search for understanding the development of human behaviour and experience."
Proshansky and Fabian[10]

In a chapter entitled 'The Development of Place Identity in the Child', in the exemplary work *Spaces for Children - The Built Environment and Child Development*[10], Proshansky and Fabian describe place identity as the "physical-world socialisation of the child". They suggest that place identity is "a substructure of the person's self-identity that is comprised of cognitions about the physical environment that also serve to define who the person is". Proshansky and Fabian discuss the ways in which children look at the environment in terms of its physical and social meanings in order to understand their surroundings, to satisfy their needs and in so doing learn to behave appropriately. They believe that the ability to 'read' environments and to form concepts about place-identity is essential to a child's development of a sense of competance and control of the physical world, which is in turn an important aspect of self-identity.

The authors further suggest that place identity is heavily influenced by the social meanings that are attached to spaces and places by other people, and that these are influential in forming the 'lenses' through which children later recognise, evaluate and manipulate physical spaces and places. From this it would seem that the semiotics of environments are not only influential in terms of children's understanding of place identity, but also in the development of the child's sense of self-identity.

2.4 THE INFLUENCE OF CULTURE ON CHILDREN'S USE OF THE EXTERNAL ENVIRONMENT

The wealth of evidence relating the influence of culture on the way children use the external environment prevents a thorough discussion of the subject here, but it is interesting to note the degree of unanimity expressed by those who have studied the subject in depth, despite their different academic approaches and backgrounds.

In various references, Rapoport explores the effect of 'enculturation' on child-environment relationships and suggests that symbolic messages and meanings within culture have considerable bearing on children's environmental experiences. An interesting perspective on the extent of cultural influence is provided by those who have studied children and childhood in different parts of the world (see for example Tuan[11]).

An excellent discussion of the work of these authors and others is presented by M. H. Matthews in *Making Sense of Place*[12]. In addition to the cultural significance of place experience, Matthews explores many other aspects, including the development of environmental capability, competance and cognition.

Another major source of information for those interested in children and the environment generally is the journal called *Children's Environments Quarterly (CEQ)*. Published by the Children's Environments Research Group based at The City University of New York, this journal has for many years been a most influential vehicle for those involved with and concerned about children's environmental experience and opportunity. The journal proved invaluable in our review of research and extracts are referred to throughout this document.

"What these studies suggest is that children's environmental transactions are set within a societal context defined and shaped by varying cultural systems. Accordingly, the opportunities that children have to make sense of place and space are often beyond their control. Not only is their outdoor behaviour constrained by cultural expectation, but also many of the artefacts of place are products of these same cultural mores. Clearly structures of this kind have a significant effect upon environmental knowing."
Matthews[12]

2.5 PLAY AND THE EXTERNAL ENVIRONMENT

In considering children's use of the external environment, play is obviously an important element. It is beyond the scope of this document to explore the purpose, function and value of play in any depth, but acceptance that play is an integral element of childhood is assumed.

There are, however, a number of key factors related to play which were central to this study.

i)   Play is a complex subject but a common phenomenon. In a fascinating article entitled 'Where did you go? The forest. What did you see? Nothing.'[13] Lynda Schneekloth suggests that the "invisibility of vegetation" is culturally based. She believes that children's attitudes to vegetation as 'nothing' reflects their understanding of the cultural messages they receive and concludes that our culture tends to devalue common, everyday elements. Coupled with the complexity of play, perhaps this partly explains why play has become so devalued within our culture and why there exists such confusion and misconception about what play is (and is not), particularly in relation to children's use of the external environment.

Thus, whilst some definitions of play might serve adequately to describe the breadth and scope of functions, needs and opportunities integral to children's use of the external environment, the term has become so widely abused that it was not possible to rely solely upon it as a basis for our research.

ii)   A great deal of research material and data exists on the provision of playgrounds for children. Although much of this was considered in our review of research, it is important to stress that our primary consideration was to discover how children relate to the external environment in general. This distinction is important for two reasons.

Brief summary of existing research review

First, there is an important point of principle here which is central to the integrity of this study. Colin Ward puts it well in his excellent work *The Child in the City*[14], when he says "I don't want a Childhood City. I want a place where children live in the same world as I do."

Children are part of society and have a right to expect that the environment in which they grow up takes at least some account of their existence and particular needs. It is essential to understand these needs in the context of the real world environment in which they live (rather than a manufactured element of it) to appreciate fully the significance of external environmental experience for children.

Secondly, considerable evidence exists to show that typically, the design of playgrounds has not proved successful in meeting children's needs in terms of play (however this is understood), and certainly provides no substitute for meaningful external environmental experience.

In many cases, manufactured provision for children which purports to substitute for their loss of free access to the external environment has resulted in the creation of places which too often provide little more than amusement and diversion. Having been designed to meet the lowest possible common denominator in terms of functional value, they show little regard for, or understanding of, the broad range of children's needs in terms of environmental experience.

From our review of research, the regularity with which this view is expressed is somewhat alarming, particularly given that it emanates from those involved in a wide and diverse range of fields of interest. Furthermore, protagonists have been warning for many years of the deep and serious harm which this approach inflicts upon successive generations of children.

"One thing that observation of the behaviour of children makes clear, though it has only recently entered the world of reports and textbooks, and has yet to affect environmental policies is that children will play everywhere and with anything. The provision that is made for their needs operates on one plane, but children operate on another." Ward[14]

"Playgrounds around the world are littered with abandoned, rusting rocking ducks and lonely chipped concrete turtles." Shaw[15]

"The majority of existing playgrounds are still of the level asphalt type, with fixed equipment bought from an ironmongers catalogue. Rarely is there grass or trees or flowers or animals or any beauty. Children are increasingly condemned to live in a harsh, stark desert of hard surfacing. This antiseptic approach kills play stone dead." Lady Allen[16]

In her classic book *Planning for Play*[16], Lady Marjorie Allen of Hurtwood, a landscape architect by profession and lifelong campaigner in the field of children's play, suggests "this arrogance, this paucity of invention, represents a world wide disease and is one of the tragedies of affluence".

Concern for the effect of the innappropriateness of external environmental experience led Ed Berman, founder of the Inter Action Trust, to exclaim in 1973 that "We are cramming children into concrete and macadam pressure cookers and we'll be lucky to produce weeds, let alone developed individuals".[17]

The difficulty of assessing the real value and meaning of external environmental experience for children is well described in an article by Brian Little, entitled 'The social ecology of children's nothings'[18]. Little explores what he calls "Sweet Nothings" or "the more subtle shadings of children's environmental experience" i.e., that aspect of childhood which often appears, to adults, to have no apparent function at all. He suggests that far from being devoid of purpose, these transactions are "the pleasant, casual, seemingly inconsequential exchanges between children and their environment that give quiet delight but which, upon request for explication and rationale, appear frivolous or silly". He urges that for those researchers seeking to draw conclusions about environmental experience in childhood, "it is mandatory to inquire into their own particular system of constructs", in other words to attempt to understand the child's perspective.

The indefinable aspects of child-environment interactions described by Little as "childhood nothings" evidently presents problems for researchers. It was therefore surprising to discover in our review of research, how relatively rarely researchers have sought reference to and involvement of children in order to understand better the subject of child-environment relations.

2.6 CHILDREN'S VIEWS AND PREFERENCES IN TERMS OF EXTERNAL ENVIRONMENTS

Whilst we have already observed that much data claiming to present findings related to children and the external environment excludes involvement by children, fortunately some exemplary and remarkable work has been undertaken in which children's involvement has been the central and guiding focus.

Of particular note in this context is the work of Roger Hart and Robin Moore. Hart's research in the early 1970s, culminating in the publication of *Children's Experience of Place*[19], represents one of the earliest and most comprehensive studies of children's own views and experiences of the external environment. This work not only provides invaluable insight into the way the children involved, used and related to the world around them, but it also explains the range of useful and replicable research methods Hart devised in order to undertake the study. (This is further explored in Section Three, Chapter One.) In addition this book contains a most comprehensive review of relevant publications which, despite its age, is still a valuable and useful reference point.

In *Childhood's Domain - play and place in child development*[20], Robin Moore reports on his research, conducted in Britain during 1975, which investigated children's specific interactions with their external surroundings. Moore states that an aim of this work was to present a case "for regarding the quality of the physical environment as a significant factor in child development - for the benefit of both children and biosphere". In addition to recording, in detail and with great integrity, the experiences of children involved, the book presents compelling arguments for an urgent review of priorities in terms of environmental planning, design and management, and proposes various strategies to effect change in policy direction.

Additional work by Moore is referred to throughout this document.

"It must be noted that many aspects of the experience of place cannot be discovered by geographical or psychological methods nor in fact by any formal procedure. We must recall it ourselves or rediscover it through empathy with children. In this way we may be able to better understand how particular places are contacted, enter consciousness and are experienced. This demands that we as investigators discard for a while our reflective abstraction and engage the landscape along with the children." Hart [19]

As already mentioned above, one major source of reference material relating to children's views and opinions of school grounds is to be found in *Ask the Kids*, which formed part of the Planning the School Site Research Project. The document records responses to a questionnaire sent in 1974 to 4,000 primary and secondary school children with the summer edition of 'Watchword', the newsletter of the children's environmental club 'WATCH'.

Despite the relatively low (7%) response, the aim of the exercise was to collect qualitative rather than quantitative data, and the publication contains a fascinating collection of extracts describing how children felt about their school grounds, what they did, what they liked, what they didn't like, and what they would change. This survey represents the most substantial study of its kind found during our review of research. Subsequently, the similarity of the children's reponses to those gathered in our own research was to prove both reassuring and disquieting given that, in the intervening decades, at least two generations of children had enjoyed or suffered similar feelings and responses.

One other source of information which provides both qualitative and quantitative data relating specifically to children's use of school grounds is recorded in *Playtime: What really happens!*[21]. This survey, conducted by BBC Schools Radio in 1984, must constitute the largest study of its kind ever undertaken. Schools were invited to complete a questionnaire to find out what children did at playtime. Over 1,000 schools responded, and in addition to completing the questionnaire children were invited to write about playtime. Approximately 30,000 children took part. Whilst the authors stress that the data should not be interpreted as definitive or scientific it nevertheless presents a substantial, interesting and sometimes humorous body of information.

Other data involving children was found but this was inconsequential for our purposes for various reasons, i.e., the sample was very small or localised; it dealt with children's activities in isolation of environmental influence or used methodology inappropriate to our own areas of interest.

3 Development of the research brief

From the review of existing research, a number of conclusions could be drawn which were fundamental to the development of the research brief.

i)   Whilst considerable evidence existed indicating the range of benefits which result from the development of school grounds, this was mainly either anecdotal or historic.

ii)   A considerable amount of valuable material was found concerning childrens environmental experience, but the majority related to non school environments.

iii)   Research relating to children's use of external environments rarely included children's own perspectives and perceptions.

iv)   No recent published data could be found which investigated children's responses to the environment of school grounds using methodology which provided reliable insight into the way the nature of the environment might influence their attitudes and behaviour.

The review of research had produced some important and very useful information. However, it also confirmed the validity of the basic question identified at the outset of the project: Does the physical environment of school grounds and the way these are managed affect children's attitude/behaviour and if so how/why?

A central theme identified from this review was the significance of culture, in terms of both the physical nature of places and the social context in which children use and relate to them. This appeared so influential that it was felt to be essential to find a research methodology which would permit adequate exploration of the true extent of this cultural influence. Having considered a range of options, it was decided to utilise semiotic research methodology and Semiotic Solutions, a leading company in this field, were engaged as consultants.

3.1 A BRIEF EXPLANATION OF THE SEMIOTIC APPROACH

Semiotics isn't so much an academic discipline like, for instance, psychology, as a theoretical approach to the study of communication and interpretation. The semiotic enterprise aims to unravel the web of shared cultural meanings that encode an expected social response to all design and its signs and symbolism.

While it is, of course, true to say that children will react psychologically as individuals to the environment of school grounds, those grounds are, by very definition of the school population, a form of mass communication — they are as much 'texts' as the books in the library, the songs at assembly and TV programmes.

In this sense, then, school grounds give out coded messages to the children who use them about their identity as part of a group of 'users'. Are they expected to be 'carers', 'big tough sports players', 'hiders and seekers', 'horticulturalists', 'confident occupiers of space', 'involved with the elements', a 'young animal', a 'socialised proto-adult' — or what ?

This structure of codes, signs and symbols makes up the semiotics of the school grounds environment. All the elements are individually 'communicating' a message to the children about the use they are 'supposed' to make of the space. How they should 'be', what they should 'do'. Trees say one thing, bushes another, grass gives a different message from tarmac, and flowers say something else again — as do broken benches, rubbish and 'piles of pooh'. Perhaps more importantly, the grounds — like all other school texts — also give out coded messages about the schools' attitude to the children. The ultra-tidy house, the house that is full of rubbish, or the house that just seems 'normal' says a great deal about how we value the people we expect to visit us. School grounds also communicate in this way.

Development of the research brief

The environment is a language with its own vocabulary and grammar. But school grounds are part of both the world of school, with its cultural and social reference points, and of the general 'outside'. Both of these worlds have set up expectations that either will or will not be met by the space itself. In other words, it is as much by the absence of 'expected' signs that the grounds will be decoded as by their presence.

In a sense then the research project became an exercise in helping children show us how they cracked the codes of their own school grounds, using the school itself – its customs, ethics and social systems – and the general outside environment as frames of reference.

To do this we used an enabling technique which we invented (now widely used in market research) in which respondents choose images from themed collages to explain what a design says about them. For instance, a tree with low, spreading branches says to children 'you are expected to climb me and have fun on me', and if children are prohibited by the school ethos from acting on that assumption then they are receiving contradictory messages; while another tree with a bare trunk says 'you can only look at me'.

Collage boards were developed to represent the symbolic universe of the school grounds and the 'outside', which gave children the imaginative tools to build their ideal environment from building blocks of cultural associations, the social system of the school – and the 'nothings' of childhood.

Virginia Valentine,
Semiotic Solutions.

3.2 THE CRITERIA FOR THE SEMIOTIC RESEARCH STUDY

Having confirmed the range of issues which needed to be addressed and the methodology to be used, we were able to determine four specific criteria as the basis for investigation:

i)   To identify what children 'read' from external environments in general.

ii)   To explore the significance of particular elements or features of external environments.

iii) To discover the semiotics of school grounds and identify whether/how this influences children's behaviour and attitude.

iv)   To consider the implications of our findings in terms of the design and management of school grounds.

3.3 METHODOLOGY

The semiotic research involved qualitative in-depth interviews with children using collage boards. A small photographic reproduction of one of the collage boards used in the study is provided at the end of this Chapter.

Group interviews with children were conducted, initially, inside the school building and recorded. The group then took the researcher on an 'expedition' of the grounds during which the interview continued. The length of group interviews varied, though none was less than an hour and a half and some extended to two and a half hours. The headteacher of each school was also interviewed and, in most cases, visits involved informal discussions with other school staff and sometimes parents.

Photographic records were taken of the grounds of each school which were all observed in use during playtime. All interviews were tape recorded and subsequently transcribed. Children were assured of the confidentiality of the exercise at the start of each interview and invited to decide whether they wished to take part – no one declined! For this reason, the names of schools visited and of children involved are not quoted in this document.

3.4   LOCATION

Interviews were conducted in twelve schools located throughout England and Wales. These were identified according to geographical and social criteria and having regard to the nature of the school grounds and surrounding environment.

3.5   SAMPLE

A total of twenty five small group interviews were conducted involving two hundred and sixteen children. The majority of groups involved children aged between 8 and 10 years of age but a number were conducted with 5 and 6 year olds and also 11 and 12 years olds. Each group consisted of between eight and ten children, selected at random but providing a balance in terms of gender. The group interviews were supported by fifteen paired depth interviews.

3.6   OTHER ELEMENTS OF THE RESEARCH PROJECT

In addition to the semiotic research, and the review of research outlined briefly above, the project overall involved a number of additional elements.

A separate study, to investigate the effect of introducing loose equipment into school grounds during playtime, was commissioned from Hull University. A brief report of the findings from this research is included in Section Three.

In addition to those schools involved in the semiotic research, many others were visited during the period of the study and the experience gained from this element of the work has been heavily drawn upon in this document. Finally, the wealth of information held by LTL enriched the knowledge base and has been absorbed into the material presented in this document.

References from section one

(1)   Adams, E. ◆ *Learning through Landscapes: The Final Report* ◆ 1990 ◆ ISBN 1 872865 01 1.

(2)   Bruce, T. ◆ *Time to Play in Early Childhood Education* ◆ 1991 ◆ Hodder & Stoughton ◆ ISBN 0 340 53878 3.

(3)   Brown, M. ◆ *Child Life in our Schools* ◆ 1906 ◆ George Philip & Son Ltd.

(4)   Boyce, E.R. ◆ *Infant School Activities* ◆ 1939 ◆ The Aberdeen University Press.

(5)   Anon ◆ *The School Site Planning Handbook* ◆ 1977 ◆ Planning the School Site Research Project, Manchester Polytechnic.

(6)   Anon ◆ *Ask the Kids* ◆ 1975 ◆ Planning the School Site Research Project ◆ ISBN 0 900313 55 2.

(7)   Cobb, E. ◆ *The Ecology of Memory in Childhood* ◆ 1977 ◆ Columbia University Press.

(8)   Chawla, Louise ◆ 'The Ecology of Environmental Memory' ◆ In *CEQ Vol.3 No.4* ◆ 1986 ◆ Children's Environments Research Group.

(9)   Relph, E. ◆ *Place and Placelessness* ◆ 1976 ◆ Pion Press, London.

(10)   Proshansky, H. and Fabian, A. ◆ 'The Development of Place Identity in the Child' ◆ In *Spaces for Children* ◆ Weinstein and David (Eds) ◆ 1987 ◆ Plenum Press ◆ ISBN 0 306 42423 1.

(11)   Tuan, Y.F. ◆ 'Children and the Natural Environment' ◆ In *Children and the Environment* ◆ Altman, I. and Wohlwill, J.F. (Eds) ◆ 1978 ◆ Plenum Press.

(12)   Matthews, M. H. ◆ *Making Sense of Place – Children's Understanding of Large-Scale Environments* ◆ 1992 ◆ Harvester Wheatsheaf, Campus 400, Maryland Avenue, Hemel Hempstead, Herts HP2 7EZ. ◆ 0 389 20987 2.

(13)   Schneekloth, L.H. ◆ 'Where did you go? The forest. What did you see? Nothing.' In *CEQ Vol.6 No.1 Children and Vegetation* ◆ Spring 1989 ◆ Children's Environments Research Group ◆ ISSN 0886 0505.

(14)   Ward, Colin ◆ *The Child in the City* ◆ 1977 ◆ Architectural Press, London ◆ ISBN 0 85139 118 4.

(15)   Shaw, Leland G. ◆ 'Designing playgrounds for able and disabled children' ◆ In *Spaces for Children* ◆ Weinstein and David (Eds) ◆ 1987 ◆ Plenum Press ◆ ISBN 0 306 42423 1.

(16)   Allen of Hurtwood, Lady Marjorie ◆ *Planning for Play* ◆ 1968 ◆ Thames and Hudson ◆ ISBN 0 500 270546 6.

(17)   Berman, Ed. ◆ In *It's Child's Play Vol.1 No.4* ◆ November 1973 ◆ The Children and Youth Action Group Trust.

(18)   Little, Brian R. ◆ 'The social ecology of children's nothings' ◆ In *EKISTICS Vol.47 No.281* ◆ March/April 1980 ◆ Athens Center of Ekistics, Athens Technical Organisation, Greece ◆ ISSN 0013 2942.

(19)   Hart, Roger ◆ *Children's Experience of Place* ◆ 1979 ◆ Irvington Publishers Inc. ◆ ISBN 0 470 99190 9.

(20)   Moore, Robin ◆ *Childhood's Domain – Play and Place in Child Development* ◆ 1986 ◆ Croom Helm Ltd. ◆ ISBN 0 85664 939 8.

(21)   Anon ◆ *Playtime: What really happens!* ◆ 1984 ◆ BBC Schools Radio.

Example of collage board

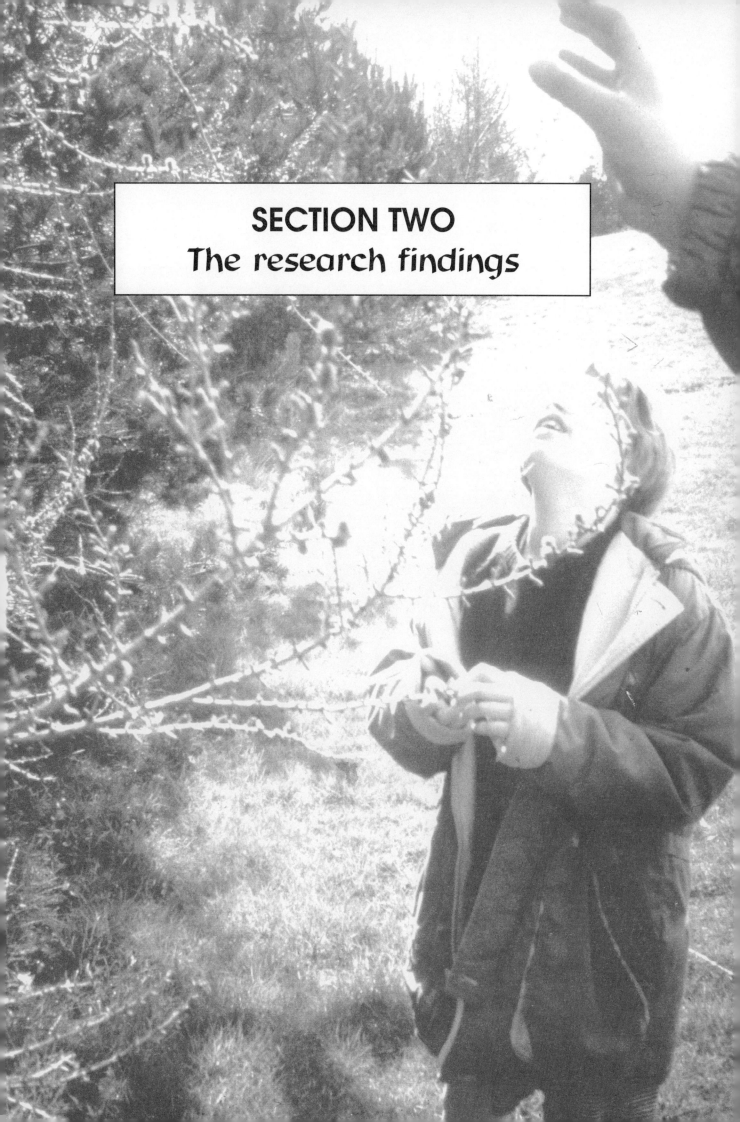

SECTION TWO
The research findings

This Section contains:

◆ An explanation of the way children involved in the study read the external environment together with a summary of their responses.

◆ How children read school grounds overall.

◆ The significance of elements of school grounds.

◆ A discussion of main findings.

...IN GENERAL

Children read external environments as a loosely connected collection of 'signifiers'. Children responded to places according to their 'potentiality' – what they might offer or 'afford', and read images of general environments by identifying sometimes quite tiny elements which, for the children, conveyed meaning or significance. In order to understand or comprehend what a place is, what it might feel like, what they could do there, they deconstructed the whole into elements with which they could identify and which for them held some meaning.

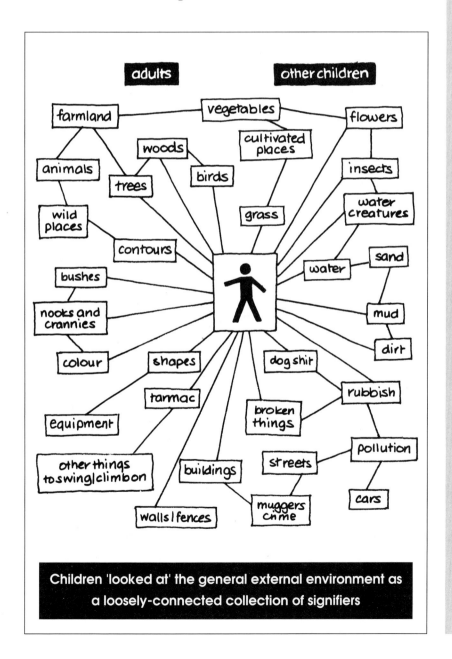

Children 'looked at' the general external environment as a loosely-connected collection of signifiers

...AS A REFLECTION OF SELF

Children read the signifiers of external environments and elements within them as a reflection of their own needs for 'being' and 'doing' and 'thinking' and 'feeling' within a cultural context. Thus, places and elements of them, conveyed messages and meanings which influenced and to a considerable extent determined the children's responses. This cultural context informed their understanding of whether a place was 'a place for them' or 'people like them' or not.

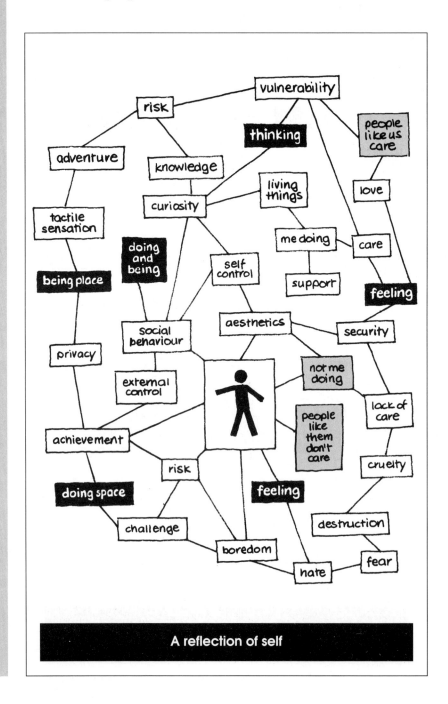

A reflection of self

How children read the external environment...

...AS ELEMENTS

Our research found that children had common responses to particular signifiers because the messages and meanings were read in a context – a cultural context – from which they formed an understanding of the place. The following table shows how certain elements of external environments were read by the children as signifiers in either positive or negative terms:

Positive Elements	Negative Elements
◆ Colour (natural)	◆ Dirt
◆ Trees	◆ Pollution
◆ Woods	◆ Rubbish
◆ Places with different levels	◆ Litter
◆ Shady areas	◆ Damaged things
◆ Leaves	◆ Colour (un-natural)
◆ Big grassy areas	◆ Tarmac
◆ Animals	◆ Animals
◆ Places you can ... climb/ hide/explore/make a den	◆ Places where you can't ...
◆ Places that challenge you	◆ Nowhere to sit/hide/shelter
◆ Places that have 'millions of bits'	◆ Places that are 'boring'
◆ Places that have wildlife	◆ Places that are too 'open'

The extent of the cultural influence in terms of the messages and meanings children read from some of the above elements is evident, for example, in terms of animals, which is why they appear on both lists. Whilst, in general, the response to animals was positive, in terms of farm animals a distinct difference emerged between different groups of children. Children in urban environments responded to such animals with disdain and often disgust, saying they were "stinky and smelly". For children from rural areas, and notably those from one school which keeps farm animals on site, this aspect of animals was unremarkable because it was part of the 'cultural norm' of their experience.

"When we go places we see lovely greens and things like that and we think why can't we be there. All we want is a better environment ... it's not too much to ask is it?"

"Once I lived in a place where there was nothing, just concrete, no parks, nothing. Everywhere you go it's either road or pavement."

"We go into the woods and build dens and swings. I like climbing, it's wicked. On a playground you know it's safe so it takes the fun out. When you're climbing a tree you can use your imagination more. Playgrounds just hinder you."

Summary

- **Children valued the external environment on a variety of levels**

On a 'macro' level, children were keenly aware of the intrinsic value of the environment in general and its importance for the survival of all living things - including themselves! They were very concerned about environmental protection and the need to care for the natural world as 'home' to other species. They valued the natural, external environment for its 'greeness', because of what it offered them, but also for the way it made them feel. Children consistently expressed very strong, positive reactions to natural areas, which they judged as "peaceful" and associated with freedom. Certain types of natural areas symbolised 'good', pollution-free environments.

- **Natural environments were preferred to built environments**

Regardless of experience, home location etc., children valued and preferred natural environments much more highly than urban, manufactured and built environments, which consistently produced negative responses.

- **Natural external environments were 'read' as places which promised to meet a range of needs which children felt to be important for them**

External environments, particularly natural environments, signified opportunities for a range of things children wanted and needed to do which were not possible indoors. For example, children always associated adventure, challenge and risk with being outdoors. Individual elements were read in terms of their interactive potential. Elements were judged according to what use children felt they could put them to. 'Found' spaces were much more highly valued than manufactured ones. Children expressed clear preferences for those areas which were not designed for them, where they were (relatively) free to claim ownership. Equally, from experience, they felt that those areas designed specifically for them rarely fulfiled their needs.

"Tarmac and concrete is boring, like seeing a film ten times."

"People don't care about the environment, not really. There's this council park, it's sort of been forgotten - it's just a mess really. There are park keepers but they don't bother about it. They should do something about it, spend some money on it, make it a nicer place."

"I don't go out much, I stay in. You can't play out in the street because of all the traffic. The parks are too dangerous. There's all that dog mess and the older ones come and there's dirty old men and drugs."

Summary

- **External environments and elements of them were judged according to the way they looked and made children feel**

The appearance of individual elements of external environments was aesthetically as important to children as the overall appearance. Children reacted very strongly to elements associated with sensory stimulus such as natural colour. For example they "hate concrete because it's boring" but flowers made them "feel cheerful". Natural areas were favoured in this regard for their intrinsic diversity and change.

- **Children were very critical of the attitudes and actions of adults in relation to the external environment in general**

Children were very conscious of the difference between places which were valued by adults and those which were not. They judged the actions and attitudes of adults and were often confused at what they perceived to be double standards. In general children were highly critical of adults' lack of care for the natural world and the quality of particular environments. They were often angry about what they perceived as adult lack of preparedness to exercise control, to maintain and care for places children knew/used/visited.

- **Access to preferred external environments varied considerably according to where the children lived**

In the main, children living in rural areas had far greater freedom and independent mobility than those living in towns. However, some children living in inner city areas had considerable freedom to roam at a very early age. Children's freedom of access, their degree of independent mobility and thus access to the external environment is controlled by adults and dependent largely on cultural considerations. Children set great store by being allowed to go out alone. This was indicative for them of being trusted by adults, a confirmation of their autonomy and, they felt, good for their self confidence. However, some children living on the periphery of large cities expressed considerable fear and anxiety about going out and believed that many places, such as local parks, were not safe.

29

"The space outside feels boring. There's nothing to do. You get bored with just a square of tarmac."

"This school is very, very interesting and we're very happy here."

In general

Children read images of school grounds, as with any external environment, on both a macro and a micro level. Whilst children deconstructed places to identify elements, they also read a great deal from, and into, the nature of the place overall.

When children viewed images of different types of school grounds they read the image on a range of levels according to their own needs for being, thinking, doing and feeling within a cultural context.

The stereotypical image (picture 1) was immediately recognised, even by very young children, as being a picture of school grounds and consistantly produced negative responses.

Whereas, for the majority, the image in picture 2 was unfamiliar and read as a place not for them or people like them but for those who are for some reason different.

Those children who attended schools which had grounds of a different nature - as in picture 2 - still recognised the stereo-typical image as a school playground, though they were surprised to learn that some children went to schools that had no animals or flowers or trees. They were convinced that such places could not be 'good' schools and were unanimous that they would not like to go there!

Equally, children who attended schools with stereotypical grounds were often quite shocked at the idea that some schools had gardens or kept animals. Their reactions ranged from disbelief to the assumption that such places were for children with wealthy parents or those with special needs.

However, children also judged places by reading elements, i.e. trees, as signifiers which substantially influenced their response. Thus, elements and features of school grounds were shown to be extremely important.

"I can remember when I was little I was in the playground at lunchtime and I looked up and all I could see was all these big legs walking past. I used to get really scared I would get knocked over by the ball or hit in the face."

"The thing is about sensations of touch and sound, you don't get any feedback from concrete and tarmac. But it's a lot better now because it used to be grey but now we've got the paintings."

"The only parts we can use are tarmac and concrete. We can't play football properly because you can't dive on that stuff. We can't even play leapfrog without getting told off because if people fall they might hurt themselves. We can't do much really."

Tarmac

Tarmac was symbolic of 'hard' play space and 'hard' play. Children consistently expressed the view that *it* was dangerous rather than what they did on it was dangerous! But because, in most cases, the vast majority of playtime was spent on tarmac, it was the only area children were allowed to use, they associated it with pain from falling over and having accidents.

Tarmac was also associated with aggressive games and domination of space by older/bigger children. This was often, but not exclusively, related to football. In schools where football was banned, the tarmac was still symbolic of "a dangerous place", because all the children could do on it was rush around, bang into each other, have fights and fall over.

Whilst football was enjoyed by many boys (and some girls), those who played it were also aware that this gave them territorial advantage, particularly where space was at a premium, because other children would not encroach onto the tarmac for fear of being hurt or knocked over. It was therefore a simple way of commandeering space.

Children were also consistent in the view that tarmac was grey, black, bleak, boring and ugly to look at. The fact that it yields nothing and produces no response in terms of sensations, other than pain and "getting your clothes torn", was also commented upon.

Tarmac held further symbolism. Children believed that there were alternatives to tarmac and concrete but that these were more expensive. Children often expressed the view that tarmac or concrete was all their school could afford and read from this that the tarmac was a measure of the worth of the school and of themselves as part of it.

In the majority of schools visited, the part of the school grounds used regularly by children for the Informal Curriculum was tarmac.

"Grass would be much better because when you fall over it doesn't hurt as much."

"t would be nice if they turned it all into grassland 'cos we could play rolypoly and do gymnastics and we wouldn't get cuts."

"Grass looks nicer because tarmac is black and plain."

"The thing is about grass, well it's not just grass. When you really look at it, study it, you find there's all sorts of other stuff there and it's really interesting. I don't mind grass because things grow up in it that you don't have to plant."

"We've got lots of grass but we can't use it ever. Teachers won't let us go on it because we'll make a mess."

34

Grass

Grass was symbolic of gentle game space – grass doesn't hurt as much when you fall on it. For the children, ideally, grass is for sitting and lying on, rolling on, touching and feeling, rather than just looking at.

Furthermore, grass enabled a different range of games and activities, particularly those which involve body contact. Girls seemed to be more aware of this difference than boys. However, they were also more particular about the type of grass. Apparently, for girls, long grass can have some disadvantages because if you're wearing a skirt you could get "itchy on your legs"!

Visually, grass was much favoured because the alternative children knew – tarmac – was always described as boring. Whilst flat grass was almost always preferred to flat tarmac or concrete, hills and changes in level generally, were highly favoured.

Grass was essentially symbolic of natural things which the children valued – as one child put it "it would be nice to play football on grass but then someone would come and paint all over it"! Grass also presented opportunities for finding things and held greater instrinsic value because of the potential diversity it offered.

Whilst most schools visited had grass, use of it was generally heavily restricted. In many cases this meant that children spent the majority of playtime on areas of tarmac which were often far too small to accommodate them. For the children, the fact that grass represented a better alternative, but could only be 'looked at' most of the time was a consistent source of frustration. Where children believed that the grass could not be used because it would get damaged, they read this as meaning that the grass was more important to the school than they were, particularly where playtime on tarmac was unpleasant, uncomfortable, boring and in their view dangerous.

How children read the elements as signifiers...

"Climbing trees is good if you're bored, it makes you feel good, it's a nice feeling when your belly turns over."

"If we had trees they would give us leaves and they look nicer on the ground, all shiny."

"If we didn't have no trees we're dead - they do all the air for us and stuff."

Trees

Trees were essentially symbolic of climbing. Even very young children and those who had never climbed a tree seemed able to distinguish between types which were "good climbing trees" and those which weren't! The value of trees for climbing seemed to lie in the unpredictable challenge they offer and as a result children were adamant that climbing trees was quite a different experience from climbing play equipment.

Children were very affected by the appearance of trees. Some types were generally felt to be "spooky" and "scary". The fact that trees change in shape and colour was appreciated by children as a constant source of stimulus.

Trees were also highly appreciated because they provide shade and shelter and "bits" you can collect and do things with.

Children were keenly aware of trees as living things and of the symbiotic and ecological significance of trees. For many this was expressed as a need actively to care for and protect trees. Children from all parts of the country spoke of broken branches being "like having your arm broken". However, even this deep concern did not over-ride the sheer fun of climbing trees, though they acknowledged the need to take care of the tree in the process!

Most of the schools visited had trees within the grounds of the school. In some cases children were forbidden to use the areas around the trees and could not therefore touch them, or sit under them.

Some schools had specifically developed areas with trees, in one case, creating a classroom in a wood. Others had no trees in the grounds at all.

"Flowers are pretty, they decorate the place up. They glow and shine and cheer you up when it's a miserable day. They brighten your eyes up. Flowers are nice to touch. They kiss your fingers."

"Just looking at flowers we get a happy feeling because everything is growing. Beautiful things like flowers make you feel comfortable."

"The flowers make it more attractive and more popular with the kids - if it's nicer to look at it gives you a nice feeling. Flowers give the school a good image."

"Plants and flowers would make the place better. At the moment there's nothing there to make it look good, it looks scruffy and has looked like that for ages so people get used to it. If there was plants they would look at it differently. If they planted the flowers themselves, they would look after it more, they would treat it like their own garden."

Flowers

Flowers were symbolic of aesthetic values. Children were very aware of the range of sensory responses and stimulation which flowers gave them and valued them highly. The relationship between the way flowers look and the way they made children feel was very strong though this applied only to coloured flowers – dull, dark, green plants and bushes were not valued in the same way. Flowers had greater status than weeds or other plants.

Flowers were also symbolic of the degree to which the grounds (and the school) were cared for. Where these were planted by 'the gardeners' children appreciated them so long as they were not planted in "silly places where you can't help but trample them". Having flowers that were planted by someone else was better than no flowers at all!

However, where children had been involved in planting and tending flowers, their sense of pride and ownership became symbolic of their relationship with the school as a whole. The majority were deeply committed to caring for their garden or plot or planter, expressing pride in what they had done, excitement in watching the flowers grow and sharing in what they felt to be an enhanced image for the school. This level of participation was symbolic of real owner-ship, that the grounds were 'theirs', that the school had vested a degree of trust and responsibility in them.

However, it was clearly important that once begun, opportunities for this level of involvement were continued. Where this was not the case, children concluded that the school's interest had been superficial and tokenist. Such situations caused children to feel confused and even angry, and were possibily quite damaging in the long term.

Most schools visited had few flowers, either because none had been planted or they had been vandalised. Where flowers did exist, the children had not planted them. In one school children had planted flowers and the contract gardeners had dug them up. One school provided opportunity for every child to have a small garden of their own or to share – and many did!

"Mud is brilliant fun. We do lots of things with it like making mud pies. It feels good jumping in squidgy mud but it always gets you into trouble."

"Gardening is good - even pulling out weeds because you get mucky. You can put your hands in the ground and it feels really nice, it's fun - they wouldn't tell us off for that would they?"

"We've got two sandpits in school but we're not allowed to use them. There's a really big one but I've never seen the cover off, I think they have forgotten it's there. The other one is full of weeds. It's a shame."

"I wouldn't like a sandpit because sand gets everywhere, people make sandbombs and throw them at you. After a few weeks there wouldn't be any sand left in there. It's no good when there's twits around - if it was stuck to the floor it would be OK."

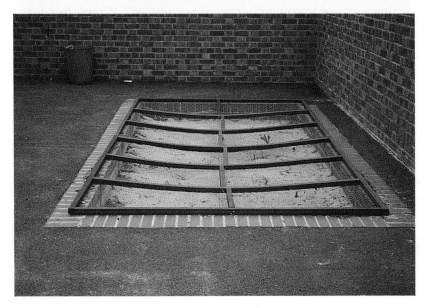

Mud and sand

Mud

Mud was symbolic of pure fun for most kids. They just loved the tactile sensation – "like jumping in puddles – it just makes you feel good".

However, for almost all the children getting dirty was synonymous with getting into trouble either in school, at home or both. Many were very inhibited by the cultural prohibition against getting dirty and a few really hated the idea of mud in their hair – and having to have it washed!

Where it was permitted, gardening was a highly prized activity, partly because it carried 'permission' to get dirty. For the children there was a clear distinction between 'good' dirty and 'bad' dirty – "smelly is bad but messy is brilliant".

Sand

Sand produced similar responses because it was usually associated with getting dirty. There was a marked difference for the children between sand on a beach and sand in sandpits; the latter being "babyish" or associated with vandalised and "spoilt" places in parks.

In most schools children had little or no access to muddy places, which either did not exist or were to be found in areas which were out of bounds. Few schools grounds had areas provided for sand – where they did these were either not used or 'disused'. In general, mud and sand and the types of activities which go with them were signifiers of prohibition and for older children associated with the nursery.

"The pond is the most interesting place in the playground - well it's the only place with living things - but we're not allowed to go there really."

"The pond would make it feel like a garden if it was bigger and clean so you could see the fish."

"We've got a pond out there but no-one ever goes to look at it. It's all bogged up now because there's no water in it ... nobody cares about it ...we're not allowed to go there and so it's just ruined ... it's a disaster area, it tells you we need help."

42

Ponds

Ponds signified care. Children recognised that ponds were for creatures (rather than for them), somewhere for living things to survive in a generally hostile environment. The younger children particularly drew clear comparisons between the vulnerability of the creatures living in the pond and themselves in the playground. Ponds therefore assumed considerable importance.

Ponds were essentially symbolic of 'the living world' for children and where they existed, ponds were the subject of much comment and conjecture. Children were fascinated with the creatures associated with ponds. On the level of 'pure child' they wanted to look and see and discover things in ponds and ideally to be able to touch them – carefully! On an intellectual level, they were aware that they should not disturb the creatures which could be easily damaged. For many, the conflict created by these two responses was quite frustrating.

We found a degree of confusion about what ponds were for and why they were there. Many children believed that unless the pond was clean and you could see fish in it either they would die or were already dead! Equally, a clean pond in which they could see fish was preferable for them to a pond which was dark and muddy.

Most of the schools visited had ponds. In the majority of cases children believed these were not properly maintained and cared for by the school either because they had been vandalised, looked overgrown and dirty or because the children had not had the opportunity to 'do things' with them. In some cases the ponds were not in a good condition, but in others children clearly had not understood the difference between a natural pond and a garden fish pond. Ponds are often located in out of the way places and where children had not been able to access them they were not conscious of anyone taking care of them. From this they seemed to draw the conclusion that the school had abandoned the pond and as a result the pond had become symbolic of adults' disregard for living things in the school grounds.

"It's good here under this bush because it's interesting and you can find things and bury things. Being in here feels like nature because of all the green stuff."

"The bushes aren't pretty but at least with them it's not all plain cement."

"The quietest bushes are the ones by the pond but we're not supposed to go there. They're good because they're big bushes and they have little holes in that people have made and you can creep in there and then close the hole up behind you."

"We're not allowed dens in school so we play hide and seek in the bushes. Why do bushes always have such big thorns?"

"Dens are places no-one else knows about, private and secret. We all need somewhere to get away from people sometimes or just to be with special friends - it makes you feel secure."

Bushes and dens

For children in our research bushes were not important as bushes but hugely important as symbols of 'the den'.

Bushes held little aesthetic value for children. They were seen as plain, green and boring, though in the absence of any other natural features in the school grounds children said they were better than nothing!

Bushes often signified 'prohibition by prickles' because their location usually indicated that an area behind or around them was 'out of bounds'.

However, bushes provided the main opportunity for children to hide and have dens – even if these were imaginary. Dens and the bushes in which they could be made were often the most highly valued features within school grounds. Dens provide privacy and a sense of security; a place where children can get away and think; a place of retreat to 'lick their wounds'; to look out from on the rest of the world.

Children all agreed that dens cannot be provided, they have to be 'found' or 'made' by the children; and whilst units such as wendy houses may function as communal, rather than personal space, they are also quite different from dens because "someone else put them there".

Essentially, dens signified the potential for ownership – that part of a public space can be made into 'my place'. This need was so strong that the ability to find places to make dens and the permission to do so, was read by children as being indicative of the school's understanding of them and their needs. Where there was nowhere to hide; to get away from conflict; to sit and ponder in relative peace; to 'do nothing'; the children felt the grounds failed to meet what, for them, was a basic and simple need.

In the majority of the schools visited, concern that supervisors should be able to see the children at all times precluded their having dens. Where bushes existed, these were often used as dens, albeit 'illegally'.

"The adventure playground is good because you don't get bored and you can play feet off the ground."

"The equipment is good but it can get boring."

"We have a professionally made climbing frame but also big and small tyres which the parents made and they're just as much fun."

"We've got this big tyre - from a tractor and that's sometimes a den, or a spaceship and sometimes a rocket ... it's fun 'cos it changes."

"They put in this trim trail on our field and now we've just got a tiny area with all these great big things around. You can't change a trim trail, can't move it, it has to stay there for ever and it takes up too much space. They say they made it for us but why did they put it so big...we all need a bunk up to get on it and then we can't get down without falling and there are all broken bricks and we hurt ourselves or tear our clothes, either way we get into trouble."

Fixed play equipment

Fixed play equipment was symbolic for the children of a recognition by the school of some of their play needs. However, the equipment itself often failed to meet these needs. Generally, the most popular equipment was that which allowed children to adapt it, to make new meanings around it and subvert or change its apparent intention. The greater the potential of the equipment or item to be changed or manipulated the better.

Children were often acutely safety conscious, aware that certain elements were dangerous or could be used in dangerous ways. However, they constantly sought challenge from fixed play equipment (as with other elements) and believed that learning to take risks was good for them. The limitations of certain items therefore led them to conclude that these were boring.

The aesthetics of fixed play equipment was also symbolic. Items painted in bright, primary colours were often read as "babyish". Items made of wood, in a landscaped, screened area were felt by some to be more interesting and less obtrusive.

Where children had been consulted, in a meaningful way, about the provision of equipment and had participated in implementing other changes to improve the quality of the grounds in general, the equipment provided seemed to hold greatest value. This may have been because the items provided were, as a result, more appropriate and relevant to the children's needs. Equally, where children were involved and had witnessed the efforts of adults in improving their playground, this conveyed messages about the extent to which they were valued which seems to have been more significant for them than the provision of the equipment per se.

Thus, in the schools visited which had fixed play equipment in the grounds DIY items were at least as popular, if not more so, than manufactured equipment. However, the context in which the equipment had been provided was found to be a very important factor.

"The seats are good - we play tuggy round them."

"You're not meant to stand on the proper bench because sir said it might fall down and a bench is for sitting on not walking on - we don't have any for walking on."

"They say don't run on the benches but there's nothing else to do."

"The benches are useless nobody uses them, there's no point in having them. You get hit by a football if you sit there."

"When it's raining we can go in the shelter. I know someone who doesn't have a shelter in their playground. I would hate to go to that school."

"It would be best if we had a shelter 'cos wet playtime is so awful but we can't play out when it rains because it makes us go all soggy."

48

Furniture and other structural features

Seats

Seats were valued where they existed in 'a place' – a nook or cranny, a micro environment of some kind. Exposed benches were used mainly as play equipment – when children could 'get away' with subverting their purpose – particularly where benches constituted the only features in an otherwise barren environment. Children often said they felt vulnerable sitting on benches in exposed locations and, in any case, traditional benches were not conducive to social activity.

Children valued places to sit *in* rather than seats and benches to sit *on*. Where they could find somewhere to sit with friends to play a game or talk, or an intimate, sheltered place to sit and 'do nothing', this signified that the grounds provided a 'place for them and people like them' by recognising and meeting some of their needs and generally making the place more comfortable.

In the schools visited, children generally sat under or on something not intended for the purpose or by the bins. Where seats and benches had been provided they were often placed in unattractive locations and were either not used or used for everything but sitting on. Where appropriate seating existed, this was heavily used and valued.

Shelter

The provision of shelter in the grounds was another element which, for the children, signified that the school and the grounds were meeting their needs. 'Wet playtime' is universally hated and children were generally unanimous in their preference to be outside rather than inside at playtime. Whilst many children said they quite liked playing in the rain, particularly "gentle rain", they were not usually allowed to do so. They were also aware of the value of shelter in providing shade from the sun.

Very few of the schools visited had shelter in the grounds. Even where extensive improvements had recently been undertaken, provision had not included shelter.

49

"It's good having animals, they're exciting, like friends. You feel more at home with the animals than you do with people, they're always there when you need them and they don't have moods. Animals are good 'cos they make you laugh."

"Animals would be good because if you had animals you'd have to have a nice environment which would be more better for us as well, but you couldn't keep animals in a place like this."

"All we have is the books to look at, now that's quite boring, but if we had animals we could feed them and look after them, study them and see how their parts work."

"Having animals would make the teachers trust us more. Animals would make it more colourful and more lively and interesting and would bring in more money. Parents would think it was a nice school with a nice atmosphere because it would be more interesting for the children."

"If we had animals the air outside would be different, it's just plain at the moment. The smell wouldn't be good and people would get germs and be ill. The animals wouldn't like the way it smells here either - all the car fumes and stuff - we don't even like it."

"My mum says animals have fleas and they make you sick."

Animals

Animals were almost universally seen as symbolic of care and one-ness with the living world. The majority of children responded to animals instinctively as things you can love, care for, stroke, cuddle, play with, feed and nurture.

On another level children viewed the idea of having animals in school as useful because they would provide an opportunity for children to study and learn about them.

For the majority of children, schools which kept animals in their grounds were symbolic of such schools being different in many ways. The existence of animals signified that children would be trusted more by teachers; that the atmosphere would be nicer; that such schools would have a better image, and that the quality of the environment would be of a higher standard. Generally, children welcomed the idea even if they believed it to be impossible!

However, some children could not begin to deal with the idea of having animals in school at all. They found it hard to believe that such places existed and couldn't imagine what a school with animals would be like.

Other children, albeit a small minority, expressed a hatred of animals believing them to be dangerous, the cause of disease, or simply that they "smell bad". Some of the children who responded positively to animals, rejected the idea of having animals in school because they would be too much trouble to look after and "too much like hard work".

Only one of the schools visited kept animals in the grounds. Whilst these pupils recognised that other schools did not have animals, they were unanimous in the view that such places couldn't be very good schools!

"The first thing I think about outside is rubbish, it's everywhere and there's all paint sprayed on the walls and lots of litter and it's terrible because of the mess."

"This place looks like a tip."

"People vandalise the school because they're jealous. It makes us annoyed and angry and upset. It makes the place look so awful from the outside."

"People damage things to hurt us because they know it's ours out there and if they spoil it they are spoiling us."

Litter/rubbish/vandalism

Litter, rubbish, vandalism, graffiti and 'dog pooh' were consistently recognised by children as signifiers of neglect.

Because children spent a great deal of time in the grounds and also because they related to places on an intimate level they were usually very aware of all these kinds of problems, down to a level of tiny detail. They could identify every cracked drain cover, hole in the tarmac, broken fence and missing litter bin lid.

The majority of children seemed genuinely distressed by places which were a mess, believing that the way the place looked reflected on them because it was their school. Many expressed the view that acts of vandalism and damage to the school grounds were a direct attack on them.

Children were particularly angry about incidents of vandalism when they believed that no-one had attempted to find the culprit or take other appropriate action. This was especially obvious where something they had been involved with in some way had been the target. They generally read this apparent lack of action as indicative that the school could not be bothered to do anything about it, rather than that nothing could be done.

Children read lack of care and maintenance of the grounds as a reflection of their own lack of value to the school.

◆ Children read school grounds as they read any external environment: as a set of symbols which tell them what they are supposed to 'be' and 'do' and 'think' and 'feel' in that place.

◆ They read the elements of school grounds as signifiers within the cultural context of the grounds being part of school.

◆ This cultural context constitutes the Hidden Curriculum of school grounds.

◆ In this study school grounds conveyed messages and meanings to children which influenced their attitude and behaviour, not just in relation to the grounds or during the time they used the grounds, but in relation to school as a whole.

◆ Thus, the Hidden Curriculum of school grounds both causes and affects children's behaviour and attitude and has considerable influence, in a range of subtle but significant ways, on the operation of schools generally.

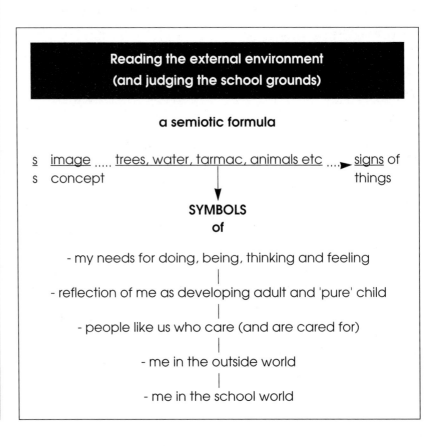

**Reading the external environment
(and judging the school grounds)**

a semiotic formula

s image ..... trees, water, tarmac, animals etc ....➤ signs of
s concept   things

SYMBOLS
of

- my needs for doing, being, thinking and feeling
|
- reflection of me as developing adult and 'pure' child
|
- people like us who care (and are cared for)
|
- me in the outside world
|
- me in the school world

3 Main findings

3.1 INTRODUCTION

This research study was driven by one main question: 'Does the design of school grounds and the way these are managed influence children's attitudes and behaviour, if so why and how?' Our findings suggest that the simple answer to the question is yes!

However, the reasons for this unequivocal statement are complex. Whilst the physical design of school grounds and the elements within them prescribed, to some extent, the way the grounds were used, children read these elements as signifiers which conveyed messages and meanings about the cultural context of the place. This cultural context – or Hidden Curriculum - was so influential that it affected children's attitude and behaviour, not only in relation to the grounds or whilst children were using them, but in terms of the school as a whole.

Our research suggests that the Hidden Curriculum of school grounds is made up of a complex web of inter-related messages and meanings which are unstated but assumed, which children read, not only from the physical aspects of the grounds but from traditions, practices and the attitudes of those around them. In other words, how the grounds are managed and maintained, the way things are 'done' or 'not done', was also seen to have considerable influence on children's attitude and behaviour.

The key aspects of the Hidden Curriculum which we believe to be both important and generally applicable are discussed below. Whilst specific reference is made in some cases to the schools visited, these are included only by way of example or elaboration. It was not the purpose of this study to investigate the schools involved, merely to use them as a vehicle for exploring a subject which has ubiquitous relevance and significance.

3.2 SCHOOL GROUNDS MATTER TO CHILDREN

As external environments, school grounds were hugely important to the children in our study for a variety of reasons. Some children had ready access to external environments of quality outside school which largely satisfied a range of needs. However, for many others, such opportunities were very limited and the grounds of their school provided their main chance to be outside on a regular basis. For these children, school grounds represented a kind of repository for all the needs which they believed could only be met by the outdoors.

Because, for many, the reasons for their restricted access and opportunity were centered upon fear, the grounds became symbolic of a safe haven in an increasingly dangerous world.

In addition to the question of opportunity it was clear that, for the children, school grounds were quite different from other types of places they knew and used. First, school grounds are generally outdoor spaces which are totally dedicated to children's use, and moreover, to use by a particular group of children over a given period of time. In this regard they are unlike any other external public space. For example, whilst playgrounds in public parks may be intended specifically for children, they do not usually provide for an exclusive or identifiable group.

Secondly, children *have* to go to school and usually have no choice but to go out into the playground or school grounds at playtime. This experience usually involves being with large numbers of other children, older, smaller, bigger and 'different' from themselves. It provides a range of (enforced) experiences outdoors which are not encountered in the same way anywhere else.

Thirdly, school grounds represent the one type of external environment to which all children have access, regardless of personal or individual circumstances.

3.3 FOR CHILDREN, SCHOOL GROUNDS ARE PART OF SCHOOL

Children viewed their school – the grounds and the buildings – as an entity, a whole unit. In this way, children's and adults' attitudes differed because for most adults, particularly teachers, 'the school' meant the buildings and the grounds were merely 'the space outside'. It was interesting to note that, where the grounds had been developed in some way, adults' attitude to this point was markedly different – the school was then seen by them as an entity.

In many cases, the grounds were used solely for playtime and were frequently referred to as 'the playground' by both adults and children. Children were very aware of the amount of time devoted each day to playtime which they valued highly, even though some disliked being in the playground sometimes.

From the children's point of view therefore, the grounds were symbolic of a place, created especially for them, in order that they might play and, furthermore, playing in the playground formed a substantial part of being at school.

Where the grounds were rarely used for any other purpose, at any other time, or by anyone other than the children, this message was further reinforced.

To the children the grounds 'belonged' to the school and by implication those who ran it were responsible for the grounds and "made it like that" for a reason. The children believed that the grounds had been designed by those who managed the school as a place for them to use.

Where, by design, the grounds met at least some of the children's needs, they read this a reflection of the fact that the school valued them and understood their needs. Where the design of grounds failed to meet their needs and playtime was an uncomfortable and often unpleasant experience, they believed that the school knew this and by implication "didn't care".

3.4 WHAT CHILDREN LOOKED FOR FROM THE GROUNDS

Children in this study had a well developed concept of their 'ideal' school grounds and broadly sought a similar range of opportunities from the environment:

◆ a place for *doing* – which offered opportunities for physical activities, for 'doing' all kinds of things, and which recognised their need to extend themselves, develop new skills, to find challenges and take risks.

◆ a place for *thinking* – which provided intellectual stimulation, things which they could discover and study and learn about by themselves and with friends, which allowed them to explore and discover and understand more about the world they live in.

◆ a place for *feeling* – which presented colour and beauty and interest, which engendered a sense of ownership and pride and belonging, in which they could be 'small' without feeling vulnerable, where they could care for the place and people in it and feel cared for themselves.

◆ a place for *being* – which allowed them to 'be' themselves, which recognised their individuality, their need to have a private persona in a public place, for privacy, for being alone and with friends, for being quiet in noise, for being a child.

Whilst these summaries are useful in describing what children sought from school grounds, it is important to note that, in their terms, children operated on all these levels simultaneously. The environment was therefore required to offer the potential for children to 'do' and 'think' and 'feel' and 'be' all at the same time.

In addition, and of over-riding importance perhaps, was the need for school grounds to be "a place for fun"!

Main findings

In terms of the design of the environment, the signifiers that tell children they are in such a place are wide and varied, but essentially they comprise:

◆ a natural landscape with trees, flowers and other things that grow

◆ animals, ponds and other living things

◆ natural colour, diversity and change

◆ surfaces which they can use which 'don't hurt'

◆ places and features to sit in, on, under, lean against, where they can find shelter and shade

◆ a landscape that provides different levels and 'nooks and crannies', where they make dens and find privacy

◆ structures, equipment and materials which can be changed, actually, or in their imagination.

The physical design of the grounds and the elements within them conveyed messages and meanings to the children about the intentions of those who managed the school in terms of what children were 'supposed' to do and not to do and how the grounds could be used. It is important to note that both the presence and absence of such elements were significant in terms of the Hidden Curriculum of school grounds.

In the majority of cases, the schools visited fell far short of the children's ideal. Mostly they offered children space for simple diversion, for what adults call 'letting off steam', and very little else. The children had therefore come to feel that the only thing they were supposed to do outside was to rush around, chasing each other or playing oganised games which largely depended on commanding territory.

Their wide range of other needs were largely ignored or prohibited either by the design of the grounds and/or by the way these were managed.

3.5 SCHOOL GROUNDS REFLECT THE ETHOS OF SCHOOLS

Our research suggests that school grounds are essentially signifiers of the ethos of schools.

Because children understood the grounds as being essentially a place for them, which they believed the school had designed for their use, the grounds were read by children as a reflection of their value to the school. Simply, if the grounds were a nice place to be, where the children felt their needs had been recognised and met, at least to some degree, which were well maintained and cared for, this symbolised that the school valued them. If on the other hand the grounds failed to meet their needs, were uncomfortable and unpleasant, children felt this was symbolic of a lack of care for them and for the environment.

School grounds were therefore also symbolic for children of the ethos of the school in terms of its concern for the environment, because to them, the grounds represented a small pocket of the natural world in the external environment. The meanings of the external environment – any external environment – and the conservation of the natural world were closely associated for most of the children in this study. They were deeply conscious of the need to care for animals, plants, trees and the 'world at large' and wanted, very badly, to play their part in this caring.

Through the formal curriculum children learned about the importance of the environment generally, about the inter-dependence of living things, about the need to care for trees "that do the air for us and stuff", and became confused when these concepts were not mirrored in the immediate envionment of the school. Where the quality and condition of the grounds did not reflect the discourse they heard in the classroom, the message they read from this was akin to 'adults say one thing but do another'. Children's acceptance of what they learned about the environment, together with their deep and instinctive need to care for living things, led some of them to question the integrity of what they were being taught and those who were teaching it.

The grounds were therefore symbolic – at a basic level – of whether the school practised what it preached and this had considerable impact on children's attitude and behaviour.

Where school grounds were used for the Formal as well as the Informal Curriculum, and adults and children had been involved together in 'caring for' and 'doing things' in and with the grounds, the most positive responses were found.

However, whilst some schools paid lip service to this need, with two notable exceptions, children were not offered any real opportunity to be involved with the grounds, to participate or to develop a sense of responsibility for the immediate environment.

From our research, participation was clearly synonymous with the development of a sense of ownership and belonging. Where children had been involved in a meaningful way with the grounds of their school, they believed that the grounds were 'theirs'. Where they had not, they said the grounds belonged to "the school" or "the council".

The issue of children's involvement and participation is one example of the way that the management policy of schools influences the Hidden Curriculum of school grounds.

Another aspect of management which was found to be very influential in terms of children's attitude and behaviour related to the way the grounds were maintained.

Children in this study were deeply affected by the condition of the grounds. In the same way that children read positive and negative signifiers in terms of the external environment in general (see Section Two), they applied basically the same judgement to school grounds.

However, because school grounds were viewed by the children as places especially for them, the negative elements of litter, graffitti, vandalism, dog faeces, smelly drains, broken fences etc., were read by children as signifiers that the school didn't care about the environment or about them.

Where children perceived that the ethos of the school demonstrated 'non-caringness' in relation to the grounds, they were faced with a difficult choice. Either they accepted this as the dominant culture and suppressed their instinctive, personal inclinations, or they rejected the school ethos and all that goes with it. For some children this led to their colluding with the uncaring attitude, for others it represented an opportunity to make a 'bad situation worse'. In some cases it was read as a clear signal, an invitation to vandalism.

In those schools where 'the school' demonstrated clearly that the grounds were valued and actively encouraged practical evidence of this, the children happily adopted this culture.

3.6   CONCLUSION

One of the main reasons for embarking upon this study was because many schools which had developed their grounds reported that, in addition to obvious and tangible benefits and improvements, the process in itself seemed to cause significant changes in relationships, attitudes and behaviour.

The actual nature of school grounds developments, the tangible outcomes which result, are of course of immense benefit. However, this study did not set out to explore or examine these in depth because this had been substantially achieved by LTL's initial research. We were concerned to understand more about those aspects which were apparently the indirect result of change.

There can be no doubt from this study that the process of development and improvement of school grounds, undertaken appropriately, is in itself the cause of wide ranging changes and benefits. Our research found that, by embarking upon such initiatives, schools had, albeit unwittingly, changed the cultural context – the Hidden Curriculum – of school grounds and it was this which brought about the intangible changes in attitude and behaviour which they had identified.

Perhaps the most important finding from this study overall is that because the Hidden Curriculum of school grounds can be identified it can be changed. The Hidden Curriculum of school grounds exists and exerts considerable influence on the attitude and behaviour of children in all schools. It is, however, within the power of those who manage schools to determine the nature of the Hidden Curriculum of their school grounds.

3.7   SUMMARY OF MAIN FINDINGS

◆   School grounds, by their design and the way they are managed, convey messages and meanings to children which influence their attitude and behaviour in a variety of ways.

◆   Children read these messages and meanings from a range of signifiers which frame the cultural context of the environment. This constitutes the Hidden Curriculum of school grounds.

◆   The Hidden Curriculum has considerable influence, in a range of subtle but significant ways, on the operation of all schools.

◆   It is within the power of those who manage schools to determine the nature of the Hidden Curriculum of their school grounds.

SECTION THREE
Implications for schools

This Section explores four key implications arising from the research:

1. School grounds, as external environments, have become increasingly important to children in modern society.

2. School grounds convey messages and meanings about the ethos of schools.

3. Children's attitudes and behaviour are determined, to a considerable extent, by the design of school grounds.

4. Children's attitude and behaviour are influenced by the way school grounds are managed.

"Children move from setting to setting and it is likely that their experience in one environment will influence their behaviour in another."
Weinstein and David

This Chapter explores the following issues:

◆ The external environment provides unique opportunities for children which they enjoy.

◆ Experience of the external environment is an important part of normal human development.

◆ Children's access to external environments is limited by a range of factors outside their control.

◆ Children's access to external environments appears to be decreasing.

◆ The advent of escorting as an element of childhood.

◆ Lack of access to the external environment may be a contributory factor in the rise of more passive activities.

◆ The external environment as a locus for social interaction.

◆ Children recognise the importance and value of school grounds as external environments.

It also contains:

◆ Suggested Activities.

◆ References.

1 School grounds, as external environments, have become increasingly important to children in modern society

1.1 INTRODUCTION

Most people believe, almost instinctively, that access to the outdoors is important to and for children; that 'environmental awareness' constitutes a part of normal development for the human being, and that this is borne of experience and cannot be acquired secondhand as some form of distance learning. If such experiences and opportunities are important we need to understand why this is so; what it is about such opportunities that matter for children; what factors in their lives determine whether they do or don't have such opportunities, and what effects the lack of such opportunities may have on individuals and society as a whole in order to consider what implications all this might have for schools.

1.2 THE EXTERNAL ENVIRONMENT PROVIDES UNIQUE OPPORTUNITIES FOR CHILDREN WHICH THEY ENJOY

One of the first major studies of children's use of the external environment which involved children was conducted by Roger Hart in a typical mid-American small town in the early 1970s, and published as *Children's Experience of Place*[1]. Hart worked with children, their families and schools for more than a year, using a range of innovative methodologies in order to investigate children's spatial activity, place knowledge, place values and feelings and place use. It is impossible to summarise this seminal and comprehensive work here but it is important to record its existence because it provides an invaluable account, a radical approach and an exceptional insight into that part of childhood under consideration.

An important factor to emerge from Hart's work relates to the way research investigating children's use of and preferences for external environments is and should be conducted. Hart undertook 'place expeditions' with children and notes that this element of his research produced different outcomes from that gathered by more traditional methods.

Hart's work provides a marker against which comparisons may be drawn. The similarity between the findings of our own research and those of Hart are striking, particularly given the differences in time and culture. For example, Hart concludes that "a most important quality of children's interaction with the environment involves the finding and making of places for themselves". He goes on to urge planners and others to take due account of the fact that not only were children's opportunities for access to the external environment in general decreasing, but that the tendency to design and define special places for them often failed to meet their needs. Others who have undertaken studies of children's needs/use of external environments have consistently re-inforced this message.

It is beyond the scope of this document to explore the wider consequences of design and planning on children's lifestyle. However, it is important to draw attention to the fact that it is unwise and impractical to attempt to consider provision for children in a vacuum, to focus too tightly on any one element of children's lives in the absence of broader considerations. A wealth of material exists which shows that the tendency to compartmentalise children's lives and experience, their very existence, is failing them. As mentioned in Section One, the work of Colin Ward [2] is of particular significance in this regard because he consistently calls for an holistic approach to the consideration of children's needs as part of society. Ward has been warning, for many years, that our whole attitude to children is basically inappropriate, inadequate and ill-conceived, not only for children but for society as a whole.

School grounds are important

From our research it is clear that generally, children felt that areas and spaces specially set aside for them do not meet their needs. Formally designated, traditional play areas, where they existed and were accessible, were mostly regarded with considerable criticism. Reasons given included the fact that they were "boring"; "designed for babies"; frequented by teenagers, often damaged and poorly maintained and generally served little useful purpose. There were exceptions to this, but as a general rule, designated places for children, as they commonly experienced them, proved no substitute for unascribed, natural or 'found' places in the external environment.

The value children set upon such environments is discussed at length by Robin Moore in a number of very useful articles as well as in *Childhood's Domain*[3]. One such article[4] reports on a study Moore conducted from which he analysed the 'mention rates' of places included in children's drawings and interviews. Moore found that the most dominant reason which children gave for liking particular places was to experience the natural environment, animal life, vegetation, weather and other sensory qualities. It is interesting to note that these findings broadly correlate with those from a later study conducted in England.

From these works, our own research and a variety of other data, it seems that the majority of children enjoy access to the outdoors; that 'found' spaces are preferred to traditional, designed playground environments; that they value natural environments and places which offer variety and diversity, and which offer 'potentiality' for change and are manipulable; that they actively seek out places and elements which present opportunity for risk and challenge and that, whilst such places need to facilitate social interaction, children highly value environments which provide a degree of privacy.

"Playground's are boring, they just hinder you."

● *"Homesites and immediate surroundings together with people and vegetation had the highest mention rates.*

● *Natural elements account for over a quarter of all mentions. If open space were included, together these accounted for a third of all mention rates.*

● *Sports provision had a very modest ranking.*

● *Indoors had the lowest ranking."* Moore[4]

1.3 EXPERIENCE OF THE EXTERNAL ENVIRONMENT IS AN IMPORTANT PART OF NORMAL HUMAN DEVELOPMENT

Whilst it was outside the remit of our research to investigate individual, psychological responses to the environment in general and school grounds in particular, the effect of environmental experience on individual human development is obviously of consequence in terms of the subject under consideration.

Some aspects relating to the significance of external environmental experience on individual human development are discussed in Section One. A further area of consideration relates to what Thomas David calls 'Environmental Literacy'[5], in an article of the same name. David explains that this involves "the transformations of awareness into a critical, probing, problem-seeking attitude towards one's surroundings".

Many authors and researchers in the fields of geography, environmental psychology and cognition, believe that the development of environmental literacy is essential to the healthy development of human beings because it is "an important attribute of an autonomous, effective adult"[5].

For many who study this area, autonomy is related to the development of competances such as spatial knowledge and cognitive mapping skills. There appears to be a strong correlation between environmental literacy, autonomy and the development of self-esteem. Freedom of access to the environment, the ability to find one's way around and to feel confident in doing so, is clearly an important human need with far reaching consequences, and one which must be learned essentially through experience.

"This newly acquired literacy can be applied to situations in every setting in which the child finds himself. It is an important attribute on an autonomous, effective adult - a survival skill for a future that will be marked by rapid change and shaped by forces which often do not pause to calculate the social costs of man's adaptation to an expanding technology." David[5]

This is sometimes described as 'environmental competance' defined by Saegert and Hart[7] as "the knowledge, skill and confidence to use the environment to carry out one's own goals and to enrich one's experience". Various authors point to the importance of environmental competance, not only for the individual but for society as a whole.

"If children do not feel competent in their engagement with the environment we might reasonably assume that they are less likely to take part in changing or managing the environment when they become adults." Hart[6]

1.4 CHILDREN'S ACCESS TO EXTERNAL ENVIRONMENTS IS LIMITED BY A RANGE OF FACTORS OUTSIDE THEIR CONTROL

It is often quoted that children are the main users of the external environment. Whether or not this is true, it would appear that children's use of and access to the outdoor environment is decreasing.

One of the most comprehensive overviews of this subject is presented in a document entitled *Children's Range Behaviour*[8] in which the author finds that the following factors influence children's access to the external environment:

"The pattern of range behaviour in children, as well as having a developmental perspective, is also governed by a hotch-potch of other influences." Parkinson[8]

◆ where they live, their age and sex
◆ existence and age of siblings
◆ controls exerted by parents
◆ cultural expectations
◆ the nature of their home
◆ the existence and proximity of other children
◆ whether the outdoors is attractive
◆ whether they are temperamentally 'outdoor children'
◆ bicycle ownership.

The authors suggest that for each child the sum of these influences will differ. Whilst this is undoubtedly true, there is also evidence that some (or a combination) of these factors are commonly found to influence children's opportunity to access the external environment. Indeed, it would seem that there has been a relatively recent change in perception of what constitutes the 'norm' in terms of childhood culture in this regard.

In our research, children living in rural areas appeared to have a considerable degree of freedom to roam and range (so long as their parents knew when to expect them back or who they were with), which the children valued highly. For some, this was so much a part of their everyday lives that the idea of any restriction or prohibition on their freedom was quite difficult for them to comprehend. Equally, many children who enjoyed such freedom were acutely aware that this constituted a kind of privilege.

In the main, those living in large towns or cities were generally not allowed out after school unless they had somewhere particular to go. In addition their freedom was quite restricted during weekends or holiday times, usually by the identification of a physical boundary or limit, e.g. "not past the end of the street".

It was noticeable that some children living on the periphery of large towns and cities had less freedom than than those living in inner city areas where, even at a young age, some had vitually unresticted freedom to go out alone or with friends. This was corroborated by one headteacher who told us that it was not uncommon to see four year olds wandering the streets around her school.

There was a marked difference in terms of experience of external environments between those children who had regular holidays, visited friends in the country, had two homes etc., and those who didn't. For some children these 'advantages' compensated for their lack of regular, independant and informal access to the outdoors.

The fact that available and accessible places were often unattractive was an important factor. Children were very critical of the lack of maintenance and poor condition of many places which were intended to provide for their needs or generally designed for recreational use.

1.5 CHILDREN'S ACCESS TO EXTERNAL ENVIRONMENTS APPEARS TO BE DECREASING

The extent of change in children's freedom of access to external environments is thoroughly explored in a study entitled *One False Move - A Study of Children's Independent Mobility*[9]. This report compares findings of similar studies undertaken in 1971 and 1990, and provides evidence of a marked change in certain aspects of childhood lifestyle.

The authors identify and examine the causes and effects of this situation and find that it relates primarily to concern about traffic and fear of accidents. Parental concern about other potential dangers, such as the fear of molestation, has also resulted in a limiting of children's freedom.

Amongst a range of aspects which are considered in the study, the authors point out that over three quarters of children's waking hours every year are spent outside school. Previous generations spent much less of this time under adult surveillance. The authors conclude that the effects of this change in terms of normal development of independence and initiative are "much more likely to be adverse than beneficial – indeed many children have lost what for adults could be called a basic right".

Our own research would support these findings. Where children's access was restricted, the reasons for this were generally given as fear of traffic or strangers. In most cases children said their parents "wouldn't allow them" but the majority understood and accepted their reasons. Many children expressed real fear about going out alone or with friends, they were very conscious of problems created by traffic and often cited particular places in their neighbourhood as being really dangerous.

"In 1971, 80% of 7 and 8 year olds were allowed to go to school on their own. By 1990 this figure had dropped to 9%." Hillman et al[9]

"Transport policies in all motorised countries have been transforming the world for the benefit of motorists, but at the cost of children's freedom and independence to get about safely on their own - on foot and by the bicycle that most of them own. This has gone largely unnoticed, unremarked and unresisted. We have created a world for our children in which safety is promoted through fear." Hillman et al[9]

"I'm more restricted now than I used to be."

"I never go to the park on my own, even though it's just down the street. There have been murders."

"During 1990, 1,356 million hours were spent in Britain escorting children. The economic resource costs of this escorting, using Department of Transport methods of valuations is estimated at between £10 and £20 billion annually." Hillman et al[9]

1.6 THE ADVENT OF 'ESCORTING' AS AN ELEMENT OF CHILDHOOD

The loss of independent mobility has brought about a huge increase in the practice of 'escorting' children, both in terms of journeys to and from school and also in order that they may enjoy a range of organised out-of-school activities.

Hillman et al.[9], point out that whilst children may enjoy such opportunities, the perceived need to take children to and from particular activities represents a major change in childhood lifestyle because, for many, it replaces the ad-hoc freedom to pursue a range of activities and interests previously enjoyed by children. This is particularly significant in terms of children's access to the external environment.

1.7 LACK OF ACCESS TO THE EXTERNAL ENVIRONMENT MAY BE A CONTRIBUTORY FACTOR IN THE RISE OF MORE PASSIVE ACTIVITIES

"TV, bed, TV, school, TV, bed, TV, school, that's how it is. We don't want to become telly addicts but what else is there?"

In our research children said that they often watched television and played computer games because they were not allowed out, or because there was nowhere to go and nothing else to do.

Lack of choice may therefore be a factor in terms of the amount of time children spend watching television. Estimates vary but data exists which suggest that the average child in Britain spends three hours per day watching television[10]. One study which used a 'time-budget' formula showed that children may spend 900 hours at school but 1,200 watching television[11].

Whether children who watch three hours television a day would choose instead to engage in more active pursuits is a matter on which substantive data has not been found. What is clear is that, without the opportunity of somewhere to go and the freedom to get there, children possibly have little choice in the matter.

School grounds are important

This apparent change in childhood lifestyle, particularly in relation to the opportunities for physical activity and exercise which access to the external environment provides, is a subject which is receiving increasing attention.

A survey conducted as part of the work of The Happy Heart Project based at the School of Education at the University of Hull, found that children of primary age engaged in very little vigorous physical activity. This research 'logged' the out-of-school activities of more than 1,000 children for a total of 14,000 hours between October 1988 and July 1989[12].

Neil Armstrong of Exeter University has been conducting studies into children's fitness for many years. He has warned that children have surprisingly low levels of activity and many seldom experience the intensity and duration of exercise associated with a lower incidence of cornonary heart disease in adults.

The Fitness and Health Advisory Group report[10] states that a lack of vigorous exercise outside school hours very likely contributes to a low level of fitness in children and that "provision for exercise in schools cannot, in itself, be sufficient to compensate for this out-of-school inactivity".

From the foregoing it may be concluded that the matter of children's access to the external environment is significant for a number of reasons, not the least being their physical health and well-being.

From *Physical Activity Patterns of Primary School Children*:

● *"Half of the children took part in no vigorous physical activity.*
● *Only 1:5 children engaged in vigorous activity on more than one occasion.*
● *The longest period of continuous vigorous physical activity recorded was just 8 mins.*
● *99% watched television on at least one occasion.*
● *Almost a quarter of children's free time was spent watching television - 3,000 out of 14,000 hours."*
Sleap and Warburton[12]

1.8 THE EXTERNAL ENVIRONMENT AS A LOCUS FOR SOCIAL INTERACTION

Without extending the debate about the merits and demerits of what children watch on television, it is obvious that this is, in itself, a predominantly passive activity, essentially solitary rather than social.

The decrease in family size in the UK has limited children's opportunities for social interaction with others inside the home. Furthermore, organised, out-of-school leisure activities are no substitute for the type of informal, unsupervised social inter-action which children usually experience when 'playing-out'.

"The most precious gift we can give to the young is social space; the necessary space - or privacy - in which to become human beings." Opie

"The most important things is being with your friends."

During our research many teachers expressed concern that children today are unable to play. This is often expressed in relation to the perceived absence or reduction in the playing of traditional games. Opinions on the subject of the prevalence of traditional games varies considerably. In the well known, definitive studies conducted by Iona and Peter Opie they contend that little evidence exists for concern about the disappearance of traditional games[13]. However they point out that opportunity is essential – a view strongly supported by the children in our study.

Research conducted by Alisdair Roberts with 10 and 11 year olds in three schools in Scotland explored children's games know-ledge and range of outdoor activities. Roberts concludes[14] that children seemed to play much the same games as their parents did but that, as a result of increasing limitation on their independent mobility, the school playground constitutes children's primary social centre for such activities.

In our study, children often related 'being out' with being with friends. Many were not allowed to have friends 'in', and if they were, the numbers were usually limited. Apart from these kinds of restrictions it was obvious that for the children, 'being out' with friends presented quite different experiences and opportunities in terms of social interaction.

1.9 CHILDREN RECOGNISE THE IMPORTANCE AND VALUE OF SCHOOL GROUNDS AS EXTERNAL ENVIRONMENTS

In the majority of the schools visited in this study children were not allowed access to their school grounds out of school time. In one case, where access was allowed and the grounds had been developed to provide a 'dual use' facility, children living close to the school said they used the play area quite often. Another school, with very large grounds was 'open access' with a public right of way through it. One or two of the other schools did not, officially, allow access but the grounds were accessible either because the perimeter fence was incomplete or broken.

A few children admitted that they sometimes "got in" to school, though they knew they were not supposed to be there. Others expressed the view that it would be better if access was organised, not only because it would give them somewhere to go but because it would prevent other people from damaging the school at these times.

Some children said they would like to have access to the school grounds in the evenings, at weekends and during the holidays. These were, not surprisingly, those children who had less or very little freedom of access to other external environments, particularly environments of quality.

It was interesting that even where children felt the school grounds were boring they said they would like to be able to use them out of school time - if there was "something organised" and they could be with their friends. Where children enjoyed their school grounds, this desire was, understandly, even greater.

In either case, for the majority of children, school grounds represented a safe place to be. For those with limited access to other external environments, the grounds were even more significant, representing a kind of refuge or safe haven in an increasingly dangerous world.

"It would be good if the school was open in the evenings and at weekends and the holidays 'cos there's nowhere else to go. We're not allowed in but some boys do come in and play football and sometimes I do 'cos all my friends call me chicken if I don't so I have to do it."

"If we were allowed to we would come here in the evenings and that. It's enjoyable in the playground, if it was grass it would be better than any park because it's safe."

75

1 School grounds, as external environments, have become increasingly important to children in modern society

What do your children do outside school time?

Where do they go; what kinds of facilities exist locally which constitute external environments of quality?

Can children access these? What are their range behaviour patterns?

What do children 'get' from access to the external environment and what are they lacking?

Are the grounds available for use by others; are they accessible outside school time?

Does your school have a written policy which spells out the value of the grounds and the functions they serve?

SUGGESTED ACTIVITIES

Organise a 'time budget exercise' with children of their out-of-school activities. Perhaps space could be found to display information about local activities or groups/clubs.

Conduct a survey of local facilities and amenities. Schools in some areas work with local authorities to improve and enhance their local environment.

'Range behaviour' studies offer opportunity for mapping and other exercises.

Explore this subject with children as part of Environmental Education. Consider the physical and social aspects of your findings in relation to the use of the school grounds. Read *Childhood's Domain* for insight.

Are your school grounds a 'public' amenity - what advantages and disadvantages does this present in managing the school? Are children permitted access outside school time? If so how are the grounds used, by whom, to what extent? If not, how might this affect children, the school?

From these investigations and discussions, produce a short statement about the value of your school grounds, not only in terms of the school but also as resources within the community.

References from section three, chapter one

(1)   Hart, Roger ◆ *Children's Experience of Place* ◆ 1979 ◆ Irvington Publishers Inc. ◆
        ISBN 0 470 99190 9.

(2)   Ward, Colin ◆ *The Child in the City* ◆ 1977 ◆ Architectural Press, London ◆
        ISBN 0 85139 118 4.

(3)   Moore, Robin ◆ *Childhood's Domain - Play and Place in Child Development* ◆ 1986 ◆
        Croom Helm Ltd. ◆ ISBN 0 86664 939 8.

(4)   Moore, Robin ◆ 'Collaborating with young people to assess their landscape values' ◆
        In *EKISTICS Vol.47 No.281* ◆ March/April 1980 ◆ Athens Center of Ekistics, Athens
        Technical Organisation, Greece ◆ ISSN 0013 2942.

(5)   David, Thomas G. ◆ 'Environmental Literacy' ◆ In *School Review* ◆ August 1974 ◆
        University of Chicago Press.

(6)   Hart, R. ◆ 'Children's Participation in Planning and Design: Theory, Research and
        Practice'. ◆ In *Spaces for Children* Weinstein and David (Eds) ◆ 1987 ◆ Plenum Press ◆
        ISBN 0 306 42423 1.

(7)   Saegert, S. and Hart, R. ◆ 'The development of environmental competence in boys and
        girls' ◆ In *Play: Anthropological Perspectives* ◆ Salter, M. (Ed) 1978 ◆ Leisure Press,
        New York.

(8)   Parkinson, C. ◆ *Children's Range Behaviour* ◆ 1987 ◆ Play Board ◆ ISBN 0 948105 12 7.

(9)   Hillman, M., Adams, J., Whitelegg, J. ◆ *One False Move... A Study of Children's
        Independent Mobility* ◆ 1990 ◆ The Policy Studies Institute ◆ ISBN 0 85374 494 7.

(10)   Anon ◆ *Children's Exercise, Health and Fitness Fact Sheet* ◆ March 1988 ◆ The Sports
        Council.

(11)   Vesin, Dr. P. ◆ 'Televised Violence and Young People' ◆ In *At Play* (Journal of PlayBoard
        Northern Ireland) *No.14* ◆ June 1990.

(12)   Sleap, M., and Warburton, P. ◆ *Physical Activity Patterns of Primary School Children* ◆
        1990 ◆ The Happy Heart Project, Hull University.

(13)   Opie, Iona and Peter ◆ *The Lore and Language of Schoolchildren* ◆ 1959 ◆ Oxford
        University Press ◆ ISBN 0 19 282059 1.

(14)   Roberts, Alisdair ◆ *Out to Play: The Middle Years of Childhood* ◆ 1980 ◆ Aberdeen
        University Press ◆ ISBN 0 0802571 18 6.

CHAPTER TWO
School grounds convey messages and meanings about the ethos of schools

"A symbolic message which lies, to which the reality does not conform, is worse than no message at all."
Bettleheim

This Chapter explores the following issues:

◆ The significance of the way the grounds are used by the school.

◆ The significance of the appearance of school grounds.

◆ The relationship between the appearance of the grounds and the image of the school.

◆ The relationship between place-identity and self-identity.

◆ School ethos and the culture of care.

◆ The significance of involvement and participation.

It also contains:

◆ Suggested Activities.

◆ A Case Study - 'From Vision to Reality'.

◆ References.

2 School grounds convey messages and meanings about the ethos of schools

2.1 INTRODUCTION

As explained in the last section, our research found that whilst the physical design of school grounds determined to some extent the way children used them, their attitude and behaviour were considerably influenced by the cultural context - or Hidden Curriculum - of school grounds.

Whilst recognition of the existence of the Hidden Curriculum of school grounds is a relatively new concept, the influence of culture on children's environmental interactions generally has been widely researched and explored within a range of different disciplines, and has been shown to be of fundamental importance in a variety of ways.

The ways in which the 'nature of places' influences us are many and varied and it is difficult to separate these effects in terms of attitude and behaviour. However, for our purposes it is most convenient to discuss here some of the ways in which school grounds were symbolic, for children, of the values of the school and how this affected their attitudes. The next chapter deals substantially with some of the affects on behaviour. This distinction is not intended to infer that these aspects can or should be treated separately, it is simply an effective way of presenting the material.

"Physical settings communicate symbolic messages about the intentions and values of the adults who control the setting." Proshansky and Wolfe[1]

2.2 THE SIGNIFICANCE OF THE WAY THE GROUNDS ARE USED BY THE SCHOOL

From our research, children read and understood school grounds in terms of what Relph[2] describes as "both centres of meaning and purpose".

Children understood 'their school' – the grounds and the buildings - as an entity, a whole unit. Being 'at school' for them involved being inside the building and outside in the grounds because, in most cases, the school day is divided in terms of time and use of space in this way.

Children were very aware of the amount of time they spent in the grounds. They knew precisely how much of each day was set aside for playtime. They understood that playing in the playground was something they did and adults generally didn't do and many recognised that adults, particularly teachers, didn't much care for being outside at playtime!

In our research children described what they did and wanted to do in the grounds as a mixture of doing and being and feeling and thinking, of learning and playing and studying and growing. Their distinctions between what constitutes work and play were different, in many ways, from those of most adults. Sadly, many children recognised that what adults called play was held to have little value; that work was important but play was trivial. Equally, children recognised that the places in which they work and play are often valued differently by adults. The very fact that most adults refer to school grounds as "the playground" seemed to reinforce this messages.

Research conducted by Nancy King[4] involving observations and interviews with young children to establish a definition of play from the children's perspective, highlights the significance of adult values and attitudes.

King concludes that children learn that play is not significant in the important business of the school, and that use of it as a reward or relegating it to outside areas further separates play from the central concerns of the school.

"In our scruitiny of the essays written by children and youngsters and the interviews conducted with them, we have found that they identified the environment with the entire school day. Breaks and the break-time environment are every bit as important to them as work and working facilities." EMILIA[3]

"A handbell is rung out in the playground... Let battle commence ... Two hundred children stop enjoying themselves 'working' inside and go outside to not enjoy themselves 'playing'... in this place we call school, there is a sharp divide between the energy we put into providing a stimulating environment for learning inside the building and the disinterest we afford to the outdoor environment, after all that's only the place where the children play."
Mrs. Z. Rydderch-Evans, Head, Cowick First School

In those schools we visited where the grounds were used mainly by children for play during playtime, the 'meaning and purpose' of the grounds was, for them, simply that – a 'playground'. It was interesting to note the number of times children remarked that teachers mainly used the playground for parking their cars!

However, where the grounds or parts of them were used as a resource during lesson time, where teachers were active in using the grounds, the meaning and purpose of the grounds for the children was found to be substantially different.

Where the grounds were not used for Formal Curriculum activities children sometimes found it hard to understand the logic applied by the school, particularly where the grounds contained resources which seemed to them to be useful. In such cases they drew conclusions that the grounds were not useful as a resource for work and were therefore diminished in value.

For many children the meaning and purpose of school grounds was defined (limited and constrained) by the way the school used and allowed them to use the grounds, because this was a reflection of the value placed upon the space by the school.

2.3   THE SIGNIFICANCE OF THE APPEARANCE OF SCHOOL GROUNDS

From our research the appearance of school grounds – the way they looked - affected children in a variety of ways. This could be described as an aesthetic response, if this is understood to mean perception through the senses, rather than simply an appreciation of beauty. In an article which explores the significance of aesthetic experience, Eileen Adams draws attention to the fact that this term has become commonly linked with the concept of beauty, whereas in fact "all encounters with the environment are the results in the first place of a myriad of sensory stimuli"[5].

"They use our playground for parking in so if we put anything in the playground they would just run over it."

"Look at all those trees over there. We do projects on trees but we have to go about a mile away when we've got millions of trees here. Why can't we just go down there and do it, it's so silly."

"Although beautification of dwellings preoccupies many a homemaker, comparable consideration is rarely given to child-care spaces. These settings, by virtue of their anonymous ownership and limited financial resources, become an aesthetic no-man's-land designed more to assist the custodian who maintains them than the users who must grow within them." Olds[6]

"It used to be just a playground with nothing in it just dirt. I felt it was saying: give me something to brighten me up, give me something to make me look better, I don't look very good like this, just a stretch of concrete."

The aesthetic quality of places is widely recognised as having considerable impact on children's feelings. Children, particularly young children, seem to be especially receptive to the sensory stimulation provided by the aesthetics of environments and elements of environments, and in this sense, as Olds[6] explains, environments are potent purveyors of stimulation and can't be neutral.

It is important to note here that our findings broadly concur with a range of findings from other research in concluding that children are responsive to all sensory stimuli – positive and negative: they do not only recognise and respond to elements which engender positive responses but are equally receptive to stimuli which provoke negative responses.

In terms of school grounds, children responded to the appearance of the place on one very simplistic level, according to whether it provided any degree of sensory stimulation. As a result, almost any element was valued if it introduced some stimulus or diversity in an otherwise barren environment. Colour, particularly natural colour, was important in this regard. The significance of flowers, discussed earlier, reveals the extent to which appearance impacted upon the children's feelings. It is interesting that, whilst we didn't set out to determine any degree of gender distinction, generally boys seemed to be as affected by the appearance of the environment as girls. On another level children were aware that flowers did not grow 'naturally' in the stereotypical school playground. The presence of flowers therefore signified that someone had taken a positive decision to put them there, and this was read by children as being indicative that the school cared about the appearance of the grounds.

Moore and others conclude that one of the reasons children value natural environments is the fact that these provide inherent aesthetic diversity and change.

School grounds and the ethos of schools

In an article entitled 'Nature as healer'[7], Olds reports on research which explored the impact of different types of environments on the health and well-being of both adults and children. She concludes that "adults' strong images of the healing capacity of natural spaces argues for increasing children's contact with nature as a critical resource for healthy growth and development."

Children in our research had a remarkably consistent sense of aesthetic quality. As already discussed, natural environments and places were considered "beautiful", whereas man-made, built environments were regarded as "ugly".

Furthermore, children were not necessarily impressed with 'designed aesthetics', particularly where these involved the use of primary colours and murals. Primary colours were felt by many to be symbolic of "babyish" things. Moreover, whilst children valued structures, sculpture and murals which they judged to be beautiful and works of art created by someone else, or indeed those which they had done or participated in doing, they were generally scathing about murals which were painted by adults "to look as though" they had been painted by children.

The appearance and quality of the grounds as judged by children was also important for them because they believed this conveyed messages and meanings about the quality of the school as a whole.

2.4 THE RELATIONSHIP BETWEEN THE APPEARANCE OF THE GROUNDS AND THE IMAGE OF THE SCHOOL

Children were very aware of the image which school grounds gave the school and felt that this reflected upon them as part of the school. They believed that because most people don't see the inside of the school and what happens there, they would judge the school and the children in it by the way the place appeared from the outside.

"Given the exquisite beauty and therapeutic benefits of nature, I doubt that we can afford not to provide our sensitive and vulnerable children, increasingly bombarded by chaotic, artifical, poorly-integrated and ugly settings with more aesthetically pleasing outdoor places." Olds[7]

"A lot of money was spent on painting on a wall but the little children take no notice of it, the only people who respect it are parents as they think their children learnt the ABC from it but it's just a waste of time. This artist came and tried to make it look like we did it - even I could have done better than that - what a waste of money."

"The thing is, if somebody looked at this school and the playground with just plain cement they will think it's not much of a place. If it looked better they'd think it was a better school. But there's no money - there is for carpet but not for the playground. Maybe it's not the money, maybe they think it's good enough for us."

83

The extent to which the appearance of the grounds and the image of the school was significant became evident in our study because it involved some schools which had made recent changes to their grounds and children were therefore aware of the contrast.

In one school, where the grounds had been changed by the addition of some imaginative and interesting floor murals on the tarmac and the creation of a small garden along one boundary wall, the children were convinced that this had had a major affect on local opinion and parental attitude. This reaction was not based solely on appearance. They believed that the fact that adults had invested considerable time and effort in the venture, coupled with the value of the garden as an entity in its own right, were indicative (for them and the world at large) that theirs was a "good school". However, the visual improvement was still a factor for them, because they believed that adults judge and value things and places by the way they look.

The appearance of school grounds was also symbolic for children of the way the school valued them – a reflection of self. Because most children believed that the grounds had been created – 'put there' – for them, if the place was "ugly" or "boring" or "gross", this was read by the children as a reflection of the way the school felt about them.

2.5 THE RELATIONSHIP BETWEEN PLACE-IDENTITY AND SELF-IDENTITY

The relationship between the quality, nature and function of places – place-identity – and self-identity is a subject explored by many researchers and has been shown to have complex and wide ranging implications. Proshansky and Fabian[8] explore the ways in which experience of place and the inter-relationship of places, affect children's development in terms of their sense of competance, independence and self-assurance about the physical world.

"Before the work parents used to send their children to other schools. Now they're staying here because parents think if the school is going to do projects like this, their children must be getting a good education. People with younger ones might decide not to move because it's a good school. Even people passing the gate think it's a nice school."

School grounds and the ethos of schools

They suggest that place identity consists of 'accumulated cognitions' about the physical world in which the child lives, which consist of thoughts, beliefs, values and preferences relating to a particular setting or type of setting, e.g. home or school, and the relationship between these settings. It is more than interesting to note the correlation between their assertions of the link between place-identity and self-identity and the findings from our own research. Proshansky and Fabian contest that children's sense of personal identity is influenced not only by the physical setting but also by the cultural implications surrounding places and that this can have both positive and negative effects.

Because children understand school grounds as places created especially for them, this inter-relationship between place and self-identity may be of greater significance than has previously been realised. If, as these authors and others suggest (see Chawla in Section One), place identity can range from affection to aversion, children's responses to school grounds may be of deep significance. For example, where the nature of school grounds produces responses which constitute affection, this is likely to be beneficial in terms of the way children feel about the school and about themselves. Likewise, responses which constitute ambivalence or rejection are likely to have negative effects on children, not only in terms of the identity of the place as a whole (i.e. the school), but also in terms of their sense of self-identity and their relationship with the place.

Proshanksy and Fabian further suggest that "inconsistencies in the child's relationship to the physical environment can lead to some degree of tension and frustration". From our research this was undoubtedly true. Many children rejected both the physical nature of the grounds and the cultural identity of the place. They didn't like the way the grounds looked or the limitations which, by their very nature, the grounds imposed upon them in terms of what they were able to 'do' and 'be'.

"Cognitions that form the basis of place-identity include affective responses to settings that range from attachment to aversion. Consequently self-identity is informed by cognitions of the physical world that are not only self-enhancing and supporting but also threatening and potentially damaging as well.

The child necessarily develops a sense of who he or she is - defined not only by an array of specific physical settings but no less significantly by the social definitions of those settings as expressed by the other people, the activities and the roles the child must play in them." Proshansky and Fabian[8]

"They say it's our school but we're not allowed to do anything. They say we would ruin it if we did but we wouldn't. We'd feel good about ourselves if we'd done something for conservation and for the school."

85

"This is a brilliant school. The animals give it a good image because we care for them and they mean a lot to everybody. You never feel alone here."

This clearly set up considerable tensions for children because generally they have no choice in terms of using the grounds: they are required to be there; they have little or no power of influence over the way the grounds are, the way they look, or what can and cannot be done in them.

It is impossible to overstate the effect that this had in some cases on children's attitude and behaviour in terms of the school as a whole, the adults who manage it and on the children's own sense of self-identity. Our research would suggest that the correlation between place-identity and self-identity is very significant. Furthermore, this demonstrates clearly how the Hidden Curriculum of school grounds impacts upon the operation of all schools.

In those schools where the dominant response of the children to the grounds constituted affection, the Hidden Curriculum of school grounds signified an ethos of care for the place and the people in it.

Equally, where the dominant response constituted ambivalence or rejection, the Hidden Curriculum of school grounds was read by the children as signifying a lack of care for the place and them as part of it.

2.6 SCHOOL ETHOS AND 'THE CULTURE OF CARE'

For the children in our study, one of the ways in which the grounds conveyed messages and meanings about the values and intentions of the school, revolved around what might be called 'the culture of care'.

On one level this related to the children themselves. Where the design of the grounds met at least some of the children's needs, this was read as a reflection that the school understood and cared about them and their needs. Where the grounds failed to meet their needs and playtime was an unpleasant and uncomfortable experience, children believed the school knew this but "didn't care".

School grounds and the ethos of schools

The relevance of the culture of care in terms of the design of school grounds is discussed in more detail in the next chapter.

Another way in which school grounds were important signifiers of the ethos of the school in terms of the culture of care, related to the way children perceived school grounds as part of the natural world.

As discussed in Section Two, to the children in our study, school grounds represented small pockets of the natural world in the external environment. They were deeply conscious of the need to care for animals, plants, trees and the environment generally and badly wanted to play their part in this caring.

In this regard our research supports a good deal of exisiting data. For example, research conducted by The Henley Centre for Forecasting commissioned by BT[(9)] concludes that children who are aware of local environmental issues tend to have a higher interest in the environment generally and are more likely to do something about them.

Because children in our research learned about the importance of the environment through the Formal Curriculum, they became confused when the theory of what they learned was not mirrored in the immediate environment of the school grounds. The messages they read from this were akin to 'adults say one thing but do another'. The children's often deep and instinctive need to care for living things led them to question the integrity of what they were being taught and those who were teaching it.

Two of the elements of school grounds most commonly identified by children as symbolic of school ethos in terms of care for the environment were ponds and conservation areas. As discussed in Section Two, whilst the majority of schools in our research had ponds in the grounds, by and large the children believed that these were symbolic of the school's lack of care for the natural world.

"The environment is a key concern to young people in comparison with other concerns."
The Henley Centre[(9)]

"We've got this conservation bit but it's a joke. It's never used and no-one cleans it up. Anyway, it's not used for work, it's just a bit of rubbish."

2.7 THE SIGNIFICANCE OF INVOLVEMENT AND PARTICIPATION

The matter of children's involvement and participation may be seen to influence their attitude and behaviour in a number of ways and for a variety of reasons.

Certainly the use of the grounds for the formal curriculum will enhance and extend opportunities for teaching all the subjects within the National Curriculum, and offers lots of opportunities for involving children (and teachers) in doing things in and with the grounds. We have already discussed some of the ways that this will change people's attitudes to the grounds.

In addition, where school grounds improvements are planned, participation by children is likely to lead to the design of the grounds being more appropriate and this, in itself, means that children are likely to develop a different attitude to the place.

However, changes in children's attitudes and behaviour which result from their greater involvement and participation do not only relate to the physical alterations and outcomes. Our research and that of many others suggests that the causes and the benefits are far more wide ranging.

In *Discipline in Schools*, commonly known as the Elton Report[10], the matter of participation and ownership is clearly recognised as influential in terms of pupils' behaviour.

Research conducted throughout the world consistently finds that the involvement of children and young people in projects leads to a sense of responsibility for the maintenance, care and protection of that which has been created.

From our analysis of children's responses and views it would appear that one critical element of participation and involvement is that this is evidence, for the children, that they are trusted and their opinions are valued by the school. Children were very clear about the importance of being involved, of doing things themselves; and this in itself made them "proud" of the outcome, almost regardless of how good it was.

"Where pupils are provided with a pleasant environment they respect it and when they have contributed to it they treat it as their own. This applies to buildings, grounds and equipment. We believe that this sense of participation in the ownership of a school plays an important role in the way pupils behave."
The Elton Report[10]

"It's a very slight difference but if people are involved they understand. It wouldn't feel the same if other people had done it. We feel proud of what we did. It's important that everybody gets to do something or else it won't work for them if they didn't put any work into it."

School grounds and the ethos of schools

Where children had been offered such opportunity, their attitude to the school and their view of the school's attitude towards them was markedly more positive.

However, children became extremely critical where they believed that they had not been taken seriously or that the exercise of involving them was 'tokenist'. In our research this was often expressed where children had been involved in fund-raising events, but felt that their views and opinions had not been adequately considered in terms of the way the funds were spent.

In a recent report by Roger Hart[11] about children's participation, he develops and expands the concept of the 'Ladder of Participation' originally conceived by Sherry Arnstein (1969).

Hart discusses each element of the ladder of participation in some detail in the report and includes examples of projects undertaken by organisations working with children throughout the world. Many of the examples in the report involve schools and there is a detailed discussion of work in schools in the UK.

Hart asserts that the benefits of participation by children are much greater than simply making the product or programme more appropriate for the user. He believes that real long term benefits lay in the fact that the individuals involved develop confidence and competences and that the organisation's structure and function is improved.

Overwhelming evidence exists from schools of the benefits which result from increased involvement and participation by pupils in terms of the use, design and management of school grounds. Any number of case studies exist which testify to the fact that the real benefit in changing the way school grounds are designed/used/managed results from the process of change because of the influence this has on the ethos of the school and the Hidden Curriculum of school grounds.

"We did tell them what we wanted but they didn't listen - they never do - they might ask for our ideas but they don't really take any notice - adults do that because they're older."

"It's really irritating that we did all the running and the sponsoring but don't get a say in what we're having."

Hart's Ladder of Participation

8. Child initiated, shared decisions with adults

7. Child initiated and directed

6. Adult initiated, shared decisions with children

5. Consulted and informed

4. Assigned but informed

3. Tokenism

2. Decoration

1. Manipulation

"I know we have improved the grounds a lot and the outside now offers a great deal more than it did but none of that matters really. The real difference is the way everyone - the kids, the staff, the parents, the local community - feels about the whole school now, it's theirs and that's the result of the process, of involving them, giving them real power to decide - it's their school now and they believe it."
Mrs. N. Redfern, Head,
West Walker Primary School,
Newcastle

From our research there is evidence that where children are involved in caring for and 'doing things' in the grounds, their attitude to the school and their opinion of the school's attitude towards them was markedly more positive. However, this was not only true of the children. In most cases where children, parents and others had participated in improving or changing some aspect of the grounds, the benefits were generally felt to influence the attitudes of all those involved and thereby the ethos of the school.

2 School grounds convey messages and meanings about the ethos of schools

SUGGESTED ACTIVITIES

Help children design a questionnaire to determine how the grounds make them feel. For example, use clippings from magazines depicting feelings which places may engender such as freedom, happiness, security, adventure etc. Alternatively, help them create an 'ideal' using such images. If this appears too detailed, ask children the simple question: "Would you spend time in the grounds if you didn't have to?"

How do the teachers, dinner time supervisors, parents and governors feel about the grounds? What image do they believe the grounds give to the school? What elements do adults find attractive and unattractive? How do these compare with those identified by the children? What effect might this be having on the image and reputation of your school?

What does the local community feel about the grounds? Do they represent an oasis of the natural world in an urban desert or an urban desert in an otherwise acceptable environment? Children could devise ways of canvassing local opinion to find out how this affects the image of the school.

Use LTL's *Esso Schoolwatch* to conduct an 'audit' of the grounds. In addition to providing a means for gathering essential information, this manual is designed to involve children and teachers in investigating and exploring the grounds together and will therefore help to 'raise the profile' of the environment.

How do your pupils feel about their school grounds?

How do adults involved with the school feel about the grounds?

How significant are your school grounds to the local community?

How does the appearance of your school grounds affect the pupils? What elements do they find attractive or unattractive?

91

PART 1

School - A place to grow

10.30 a.m. A handbell is rung out in the playground, a signal that a member of staff, the preserver of health and safety for the next fifteen minutes is out in the playground. Let battle commence! Two hundred children stop enjoying themselves 'working' inside and go outside to not enjoy themselves 'playing'. Exaggeration? Yes, I admit it, a mild one. Yet in this place that we call school, there is a sharp divide between the energy we put into providing a stimulating environment for learning inside the building, and the disinterest we afford to the outdoor environment, after all that's only the place where the children play.

I am confused for throughout the twenty years of my teaching career consistent recognition has been given to the important role of play in the learning process of early childhood. Inside the building work is play, play is work. Outside play is boredom, bullying and barrenness.

Why does 'work' only take place inside? Why shouldn't the grounds of a school be seen as an integral part of an exciting environment for learning? Do we need to distinguish between work times and play times? Could we not merely recognise that we will need to vary the pace from time to time as we move through the school day? There will need to be times to be actively learning, times to be reflective, in order to allow the absorbtion and digestion of new experiences, new information.

I have been convinced for many years now that there is a consistently missed opportunity to make the grounds of a school a world in miniature, a place where discovery, exploration and enquiry can take place. Surely grounds should be planned with the same attention to detail as the school's buildings.

Cowick First School is about to be enlarged and upgraded and our grounds will be more than doubled. Schools in the secondary phase of education are often designated Community Colleges. Why shouldn't a first school be a Community School? We will be one. We'll base our planning on this premise. We'll share Christian Schiller's dream:

> "What I see, in every small community (a few streets, maybe one street) is a building, the Community's building, and it will be a place to which young children come to play, to explore, to learn. There will be facilities there far greater than can be provided in any one home. And there will be teachers there to help, teachers who are there as teachers. And mum will come there and feel at home, and dad and the neighbour next door, and they'll understand and they will help from time to time."

92

Italian gardens had fine statues in them. Our grounds must be peopled with living things in infinite variety. Shape and size won't matter, the requirements will be the ability to wander and reflect (didn't a postman discover a star), to be enthusiastic and to discuss and to answer questions.

It will help if some of our people are old with many memories to share. There must be comfortable benches in sheltered spots in our grounds for the wise ones of our community to sit on and remember their childhood, as they watch the young of today engaged in busyness. ("Share your remembering with me 'gran', I feel like a history lesson today.")

There will be an allotment in our grounds that Mr. Whats-his-name has use of. He will give us a timetable to tell us what he will be doing each week. "Why are you putting that smelly stuff on the soil?" "Ugh, fancy using that!" Organic farming will be part of our everyday life. Oh, the adjectives that we could discover when writing about the compost heap!

We'll have hens and ducks in our grounds. Rare breeds are expensive you know, a hen could cost as much as £20, and that's almost as much as a set of plastic sorting toys would cost. Why does the word 'priorities' keep coming into my mind? Why should I feel uneasily that we've not always got them right. Mrs. Forget-her-name-now, has always wanted to keep hens but there wasn't much room in her back graden. She'll be glad to share our grounds and will love to see the children's faces when the chicks emerge from the eggs.

We'll have a pen where animals can come for a holiday. Surely a donkey would enjoy a change of scenery for a week and when she has gone home we'll have a pig to stay. We'll sell the honey that's groundrent from the man who has got his beehives on our patch at the summer fete – at least we'll sell what's left when we've both tasted and cooked with it.

Our grounds must cater for people who are different. Tom's grandad now has to sit in a wheelchair all day long but he'd like to be able to grow things like he used to do. We'll make him a miniature garden where the flower beds are raised. (Strange isn't it that people who are different like to do the same things as us.) Mrs. Brown is blind, the garden that we'll make for her will be a very 'smelly' one. Our curriculum must help the children recognise that difference must be appreciated and catered for if we're all to be allowed to be the same.

We'll want a pond and an animal house to give permanent shelter to the small creatures who will always live with us. We'll need a tree nursery and the sort of area that is grandly named a three canopied habitat (trees shelter shrubs, shrubs shelter herbage), so that birds and mini-beasts will have a home with us as well.

Our mini-world, our outside-world, will concern us with Change and Cause and a seeking out of evidence. We'll learn to observe in detail. We'll grow in our ability to understand and respond to people. Our concern with our immediate community will help us to relate to the wider society to which we belong. We'll develop a sense of Sequence and of Time from which will grow our empathy.

Cynics will shake their heads and tell us that we are riding for a fall. Vandals will butcher our hens and ducks. Glue sniffers will use our quiet retreats. Promises of support will not materialise.

We'll say, if our ideals are betrayed, if tragedy intrudes, we'll grieve and grow together - in humanity.

PART 11

A discussion of changes in children's behaviour following improvements to the grounds

As a headteacher, I require of myself that I am an effective educationalist, manager and administrator, not to mention a reasonable human being. If I am to be all of these things I need to have **Playtimes**. That is, if playtimes can be interpreted as: relaxation times, choice of activity times, stimulation of a constrasting form to my work times. The 'playtimes' I require for the preservation of my own sound mental health are not: doing nothing times, being bored times, being unstimulated times. Are the needs of the children who are the pupils of Cowick First School any less than my own? If they are to achieve their full educational potential, it will only be by working very hard. It surely follows, therefore, that they too will need periods of appropriate recreation in order to re-energise.

Five years ago the playground at Cowick consisted of a walled rectangle of tarmac, similar in many ways to the exercise yards provided for convicts in Victorian prisons. Playtimes meant that for a quarter of an hour in the morning and for almost an hour at lunch time, the children were herded into this sterile space. Choice of activity was negligible. They could either attempt to play some games which required movement around this space and risk getting into trouble for knocking over those who had very little chance of getting out of their way, or squash themselves against the wall and observe the hurly burly, getting colder and colder by the minute in the winter time.

This inhumane treatment of young children resulted in aggressive behaviour on the part of some, frustration and boredom for most. Tension was very much part of the ethos of playtime and fear too was present for a proportion of our pupils. The price paid in the adverse effect on the workforce on their return to the workplace of the classroom was so high that no Managing Director worth his salt would ever contemplate it. Colleagues may think that I exaggerate or that I describe exceptional circumstances. I think that I describe playground provision which schools have been numbed into considering the norm because of the lack of both financial and physical resources.

The lack of an appropriately planned space for recreation can undoubtedly be reflected in the atmosphere and attitude of the children when they return to the classroom after playtime or the lunch hour. Bickering started outside then continues inside. A sense of aggravation is vented on a peer in a workgroup. It may be hard to concentrate when the activities of the previous hour have caused your emotions to be adversely disturbed or maybe even churned. Surely most harmful of all to the young child is the feeling of having been let down by that seemingly kind and supportive adult who you call your teacher. A teacher who on the one hand protects you from any situation in the indoor learning environment which causes you anxiety but on the other hand, daily forces you outside into the most unfriendly of environments without any support whatsoever.

Three years ago as part of an upgrading and remodelling programme the school acquired a piece of waste ground which bordered our school. Wonderously a strip of overgrown orchard was part of the rich acquisition. We were also offered the services of a talented landscape architect deeply committed to providing children with an outdoor environment which matched the richness of the internal one. Madeline Pickthorne and I exchanged ideas until we were dizzy. The budget we worked to was somewhat limited but the end result was an outdoor environment for the children which gave them personal space and choice. Now we had: an area of tarmac, a grassed area, a pond and a wild space, places where fruit bushes and flowering shrubs and trees of all kinds could grow, and the kind of grounds where birds and insects and creatures of all varieties could be encouraged to share our lives. A wonderful 'Dad' called Richard Baily created a fenced allotment for us. A thousand pounds raised by our community association funded the building of protected space and cages for rabbits and guinea pigs who will soon be joined by hens and bantams.

I believe that we now have a space where the kind of playtimes take place which offer our children opportunities for personal and social growth. The staff of the school can recognise that many of the stated objectives of the fourteenth of the HMI discussion documents 'Personal and Social Education from 5 to 16' are being achieved through our aims for recreational times.

A wide choice of activity at playtime means that the children have the opportunity to develop independence of mind. Tyron may want his friend Mark to join him in a game of football, Mark on the other hand has asked if he can clean out the rabbits. Both choose to go their own way, inspite of close friendship neither influences the other. Each boy is learning to respect another's choice. The beginnings of understanding for the needs of others is inherent in incidents of this kind.

A wide choice of activity is not without its problems. Numbers on certain activities must be limited, not everyone can have their first choice of activity each day or even their second or third choice. The children have been given the opportunity to devise rules which govern who can do what, when. So we explored the nature of rules and the need for their existence. At a level appropriate to their age our pupils are gaining knowledge and understanding of both their own and other people's rights.

Learning to stand up for their rights as far as chosen activity is concerned is, we believe, helping children to gain experience in standing up to bullies. Six year old Claire knows that a contract exists which states her right to play in the wild area on certain days and that it cannot be challenged by eight year old Andrew. She is confident that school law will support her.

The variety of playing area available within the shool grounds is helping children towards greater awareness of various conservation problems. The children know that play within the wild area needs to be rationed otherwise all the grasses get trampled before they can seed, flowers are crushed, young trees harmed.

Involving children in discussion about ideal play provision in the grounds for example, striking a balance between places where you can be active and places where you can sit and rest, has involved us in discussion about leisure provision in our city and about healthy living.

All in all each improvement in the outdoor environment of the school has brought about an enrichment in the personal and social development of the school community. At Cowick, having acknowledged that children are people with varying recreational needs, we hope we are demonstrating continually to our pupils both our concern for their well being and our recognition of individual needs. The children in turn are being made aware of the fact that different things make different people happy. In one case sitting under an apple tree and talking to a friend, in another being able to climb and jump and run. It is our hope that demonstration of concern is contagious and that thoughtfulness for the needs of others will be caught by our pupils.

The concern of the school for the children's welfare at playtime and lunchtime has obviously meant a great deal to the parent body and has helped to foster the home/school partnership. Since our battle to improve outdoor provision patently demonstrates care, the trust spreads and leads to a reciprocal attitude to our approaches to learning in the classroom. A school which obviously cares so much for

96

the well being of children is unlikely to be advocating a 'real book' approach to the teaching of reading if it is not in the best interest of the child.

We have no way of looking into the future, but we believe that children who have felt secure in their school and whose trust in the teaching staff's concern for their happiness has never been betrayed will be most unlikely to become the school vandals of the future.

Certainly we know that children who have 'played well' return to their classrooms refreshed and renewed. The happy ethos of recreational times is reflected in positive attitudes to work and towards their peers on their return to the classroom.

These two reports were written by Mrs. Zoe Rydderch-Evans, Headteacher of Cowick First School, Exeter, to whom we are most grateful for permission to reproduce them as a case study.

References from section three, chapter two

(1)   Proshansky E., and Wolfe, M. ◆ 'The physical setting and open education' ◆ In *School Review* ◆ 1974.

(2)   Relph, E. ◆ *Place and Placelessness* ◆ 1976 ◆ Pion Press, London.

(3)   Anon ◆ 'Pupils' Working Environment at School in Use' (EMILIA) ◆ In *School Research Newsletter* ◆ September 1985 ◆ Swedish National Board of Education.

(4)   King, Nancy R. ◆ 'Play: The Kindergartners' Perspective' ◆ In *The Elementary School Journal Vol.80 No.2* ◆ November 1979 ◆ The University of Chicago.

(5)   Adams, Eileen. ◆ 'Back to Basics: Aesthetic Experience' ◆ In *CEQ Vol.8 No.2 Children's Aesthetic Experience of the Environment* ◆ 1991 ◆ ISSN 0886-0505.

(6)   Olds, Anita ◆ 'Designing Settings for Infants and Toddlers' ◆ In *Spaces for Children* ◆ Weinstein and David (Eds) ◆ 1987 ◆ Plenum Press ◆ ISBN 0 306 42423 1.

(7)   Olds, Anita ◆ 'Nature as healer' ◆ In *CEQ Vol.6 No.1 Children and Vegetation* ◆ Spring 1989 ◆ Children's Environments Research Group, The City University of New York ◆ ISSN 0886 0505.

(8)   Proshansky, H. and Fabian, A. ◆ 'The Development of Place Identity in the Child' ◆ In *Spaces for Children* ◆ Weinstein and David (Eds) ◆ 1987 ◆ Plenum Press ◆ ISBN 0 306 42423 1.

(9)   Anon ◆ *Young Eyes: Children's Vision of the Future Environment* ◆ 1990 ◆ The Henley Centre for Forecasting.

(10)   Anon ◆ 'Discipline in Schools' - Report of the Committee of Enquiry chaired by Lord Elton ◆ 1989 ◆ HMSO ◆ ISBN 0 11 270665 7.

(11)   Hart, Roger ◆ *Children's Participation: From Tokenism to Citizenship - Innocenti Essays No.4* ◆ 1992 ◆ UNICEF ◆ ISBN 88 85401 05 8.

CHAPTER THREE
Children's attitude and behaviour
are determined, to a considerable
extent, by the design of school
grounds

"In any environment, both the degree of inventiveness and creativity and the possibility of discovery, are directly proportional to the number and kinds of variables in it."
Simon Nicholson

This Chapter explores the following issues:

◆ Some aspects of the influence of the design of environments on children's behaviour.

◆ The importance of environmental quality.

◆ The comfort factor.

◆ The importance of diversity, variety and manipulation.

◆ The provision of fixed play equipment.

◆ The importance of participation and involvement by children.

◆ The relationship between the design and maintenance of school grounds.

It also contains:

◆ Suggested Activities.

◆ References.

3 Children's attitude and behaviour are determined, to a considerable extent, by the design of school grounds

3.1 INTRODUCTION

As we have explained throughout this document, our research indicates that there are many ways in which school grounds influence children's attitudes and behaviour. Thus, whilst this chaper is concerned primarily with the influence of the design of school grounds, this cannot (and should not) be dealt with in isolation of other important factors.

Furthermore, it is important to point out here that our research set out to consider the broad range of ways in which the design and management of school grounds influences children's attitude and behaviour. Whilst it was obviously necessary to take account of the fact that certain parts of the grounds may have been used for particular purposes or at particular times, our concern was focussed on broad rather than particular aspects of the way the grounds influenced children's attitude and behaviour in general. It is interesting to note that the research findings supported this approach. Children viewed the grounds of their school as a whole place, an entity, rather than as separated, segregated units for use either for work or play or at particular times of the day.

The significance of elements of school grounds on children involved in our research is evident from the material contained in Section Two. The purpose of this Chapter is to consider the relevance of design in general as a determinant in children's attitude and behaviour, and to identify a number of critical factors which emerge as being relevant in consideration of the issue overall.

"Interestingly enough, both human and chimpanzee children are placed in an environment which is not 'natural' but which has been structured for them. However, the environment created for the chimpanzee was planned with more science, art and attention to their needs and potential."
Aaron and Winawer[1]

3.2 SOME ASPECTS OF THE INFLUENCE THAT THE DESIGN OF ENVIRONMENTS HAS ON CHILDREN'S BEHAVIOUR

Through our research we were able to explore the ways children used school grounds and to compare the different patterns of behaviour in relation to a wide variety of different environments. Not surprisingly, considerable differences were found between the behaviours of children in 'stereotypical' school grounds which were mainly tarmacced and featureless, and those which offered diversity and stimulation. Whilst a range of factors affect individual children's behaviour patterns, the correlation between the behaviour patterns of groups of children and the nature of the environment clearly suggests the extent to which the design of school grounds has an influence. This finding is hardly surprising. If the analogy were to be drawn with say, the classroom environment, it would be readily appreciated that better learning outcomes are achieved in a room containing an adequate range of resources and material than one which was completely bare. What is surprising is the common failure to recognise the influence of school grounds design in determining the behaviour of the children using them.

In a fascinating exploration of the role of ecological psychology in the study of children's behaviour, Paul Gump[2] discusses the concept of 'setting coercivity'. Using data gathered from an observational research study of the behaviour of children in different settings, Gump finds that several aspects of the behaviour of a child often changed dramatically as that child moved from one setting to another and, further, that the behaviours of different children in the same setting were more similar than the behaviour of any one in different settings. Gump uses this data to support his belief that settings are ecological rather than psychological or social, that the setting essentially 'has its own way'. Thus whilst the degree of individual or psychological influence may be a factor, Gump suggests that settings provide a context which, by design, determines behaviour. From his work it may also be seen that behaviour in given settings is influenced by their cultural context.

School grounds design

This concept is further explored in the same publication by Carpenter, Huston and Spera[3] who report on a study of children's time use. These researchers broaden the concept of setting coercivity by suggesting that, over time, the behaviours developed by children are partly a function of the settings in which they spend their time, and that whilst children may have a degree of choice in terms of activities, once in a given setting "there is ongoing interactive influence between aspects of the setting and the child's social and cognitive behaviours".

Another example of the way the design of environments influences children's behaviour is given in a research paper by Rothenberg, Hayward and Beasley[4]. This reports on a widely acclaimed study undertaken to compare children's behaviours in three different types of (out of school) play settings, described as "traditional, contemporary and adventure" playgrounds. The research involved behavioural mapping and behavioural setting records to establish flow, duration and content of behaviour of children. It also involved interviews with adults and children. The authors found that the design of the environment not only determined *whether* children used the facility, but also *how* they used it. Whilst this research involved non-school environments, the findings are of interest because they identify a clear correlation between design and the behaviour of children. The authors further suggest that the design of such environments has implications in terms of the degree and nature of social interaction, and that the role of adults is important in terms of children's sense of ownership and belonging.

The work of these researchers and others, clearly suggests a strong link between the design and nature of environments and the behaviour of children using them. There is no reason to believe that these findings and conclusions, drawn from research conducted in other settings, are not equally applicable to school grounds.

"The physical milieu of the behaviour setting, its social programme and participants levels of involvement encourage or coerce specific behaviours elicited by that behaviour setting. Over time, the behaviours developed by children are partly a function of the settings in which they spend their time."
Carpenter et al.[3]

"In speculating about the relationship between a child's activities and the environmental setting in which those activities occur, one frequently hears that children can 'play' in any setting. However, the data from this study indicates that... the opportunities and constraints of the physical environment predict the majority of the predominant activity."
Rothenberg et al.[4]

"The space outside feels boring, there's nothing to do."

"This place is very, very interesting."

"The playground's supposed to be something you play in, you've got to do something, you can't just sit there like a stuffed lemon."

Our own research would strongly support this view. On a very basic level, barren, featureless school grounds offering children nothing with which to interact limited their opportunities and therefore affected the way they behaved. On the other hand, where schools had developed the grounds, and designed them to reflect the purpose and function of the Informal Curriculum, the children were involved, stimulated and clearly enjoyed both the experience and the place.

Moreover, the fact that children believed, quite reasonably, that the playground was a place provided by the school for playtime, but which manifestly failed in most cases to meet their needs, left some confused and even quite angry. This affected their attitude in relation to the grounds, the school and those who ran it.

It is interesting, not to say alarming, to note the extent to which the issue of boredom arose in our research. Both children and adults recognised that boredom was often the cause of all kinds of inappropriate behaviour. However, whilst children usually related boredom to the limitations imposed by the environment in terms of its design and management, adults rarely did, citing children's "inability to play" as the cause rather than the effect of both boredom and inappropriate behaviour.

In recent years considerable attention has been focussed upon the problem of inappropriate behaviour of children, particularly in school grounds, and a great deal of material has been generated which attempts to help those who manage children at playtime to deal with inappropriate behaviour. The subject of management generally is dealt with in detail in the next chapter of this document. However, it is important to point out here that our research, and that of many others, provides strong support for the need to recognise that amongst a range of possible causes for such behaviour, the physical design and nature of the environment has significant influence.

School grounds design

One of the most comprehensive accounts of the effect of changing the design of school grounds on children's behaviour is provided by Robin Moore in 'Before and After Asphalt'[5]. Moore reports the findings of a 'postconstruction evaluation' which sought to identify the effects of developments which transformed the 'asphalt monoculture' of a 1.5 acre elementary school yard by the creation of ponds, a stream, woodland, meadow, garden and play structures.

Moore remarks that stereotypical, tarmacced school grounds are so common that the inappropriate nature of this environment for children has ceased to be remarkable to adults. The wide range of negative effects resulting from boredom experienced by children before the changes are sharply contrasted with the fun, diversity and stimulating opportunities provided subsequently. Moore comments on the fact that schools often overlook the importance of fun: "Too often adults look at fun as somehow devaluing straight-faced education. Yet it is happy times that people remember best. Laughing faces are a powerful symbol of well-being, of education too."

It is often quoted that children will play anywhere. This is undoubtedly true but the quality of the experience is widely recognised as being dependent upon the quality of the environment. School grounds offer a potentially limitless range of experiences and opportunities. However, the design of the grounds will determine what children do and are able to do in them.

The potential of school grounds is imaginatively explored in a fascinating chapter by Robin Moore entitled 'Generating Relevant Urban Childhood Places: Learning from the Yard'[6]. Using his experiences from the development of the Washington Elementary Schoolyard, Moore develops his theory of 'Behaviour/Environment Ecosytems', explaining how elements of place can be designed to provide an ideal childhood ecology.

"Boredom is the result of an absence of playing and learning opportunities. It extracts a high cost in missed learning opportunities - benefits lost forever, if not captured in early childhood. Boredom is rarely considered a social disease yet some of its crippling symptoms... are issues of national concern. Boredom negates motivation... presents a barrier to individual development, self sufficiency and social integration. Bland hard surfaces breed animosity. They injure body and spirit."
Moore[5]

"Access to a broad diversity of resources is essential to stimulate adequate play and learning behaviour. The responsibility for access and diversity rests squarely with adult institutions."
Moore[6]

Children in our research enjoyed the opportunities which the Informal Curriculum provided - a chance to be with their friends; to get a break from teachers; to be in the open air; to do things they wanted to do. However, many experienced frustration and boredom, and often severe loneliness which for them was a direct result of the sterile, barren and unresponsive nature of the environment which offered little opportunity for anything other than rushing around, or as adults often put it 'letting off steam'!

The influence of the nature of the environment on how children use it has led anthropologists such as Swartzman to point out that 'play texts', the play events themselves, cannot be fully understood in isolation from the 'play contexts', the social and physical settings in which the play occurs. All this would suggest that it is essential to ensure that "settings are conducive to mature forms of play before concluding that the lack of such play is indicative of immaturity or interpersonal dysfunctions"[7].

Research by Moore and others clearly supports our findings and the experience of many schools in concluding that children's behaviour in school grounds is determined to a considerable extent by the design of that environment.

3.3 THE IMPORTANCE OF ENVIRONMENTAL QUALITY

It is undoubtedly important that the design of school grounds reflects the functions they are required to serve. This will ideally include provision for all or at least some elements of the National Curriculum as well as for the Informal Curriculum. In addition, there are many other uses and functions which school grounds may serve, not only for pupils but for the wider community. School grounds represent a valuable community resource and, wherever possible, should offer multiple functions and uses in order that maximum possible benefit is achieved. However, in addition to functional considerations, our research suggests that there is an over-riding need for the grounds as a whole to represent environments of quality.

Children spend a great deal of their childhood in school grounds or at least in contact with them. We have already shown that for many children the grounds of the school provide the majority of their experience of the outdoors.

Many eminent researchers in the field of child-environment relations point to the importance for children of access to environments of quality. Quality is a somewhat arbitrary term, but from such material it is possible to identify a number of key elements which were mirrored in the findings of our own research and which are therefore pertinent to any discussion of the design of school grounds.

Throughout our own research children talked constantly about the way the grounds looked. As can be seen from Section Two, colour, particularly natural colour played an important part for the children in determining whether the place was "cheerful" and "interesting" or "dull" and "drab". In this regard our findings correlate with many other studies which suggest that such reponses have an impact on children's attitude and behaviour.

Robin Moore notes that the aesthetic appeal of school grounds is strong in its effect on feelings and behaviour because "emotions are stirred and spirits moved". Whilst children sometimes struggle to find the words to express such sentiments, many in our research spoke of the fact that certain environments, judged on appearance alone, felt "peaceful" and "special". They were also able to distinguish whether environments were "fun" or "exciting", or not, based on the way they looked.

3.4   THE COMFORT FACTOR

In addition to the need for the design of environments to provide specific functions and purposes, all environments provided for human beings are improved where they meet some basic human needs.

"A preliminary look at these responses suggests that there is a strong relationship between the attitudes that children have about the environment and its colourfulness. The old playground was described as 'dull', 'grey', 'plain' and 'bare' and perceived as both boring and dangerous. On the other hand the new playground was described as 'colourful', 'cheerful' and 'beautiful' and was perceived as a place in which one could feel happy." Kerns[8]

"It is important that people feel a strong sense of attachment to the places where they have to spend so much of their time. This is especially true of children and schools. Schools need to be attractive places in every sense of the word - not only with cosmetic planting along their public 'fronts' but with private 'backs' that each day make children eager to return." Moore[5]

105

In all the schools we visited children talked about getting hurt, about the pain which the grounds of the school inflicted upon them, physically. This is particularly evident in the comments in Section Two in relation to grass and tarmac. Grass was preferred by children because "it looked better" than tarmac which is grey and dull and boring but - overwhelmingly - grass was preferred because "it doesn't hurt so much if you fall on it".

It must of course be recognised that children often engage in inappropriate behaviour and it is often this, rather than the tarmac, which is actually the cause of the problem. It is further recognised that many schools have no option because the whole of the school site is tarmacced. However, where grass does exist, it must surely be questionable whether it would not be preferable for children to be able to engage in normal, childhood activities on grass and get muddy rather than a cut knee or torn clothes. For the children in our research, this aspect was paramount above all others in terms of the 'comfort factor' of school grounds.

"If children were unionized they would surely organize walk-outs and strikes against such atrocious working conditions. The fact that they are still prevalent in the majority of schools, where supposedly children should learn understanding and respect for their surroundings, is a measure of adults' disregard for children's basic right to a safe environment, one that is life enhancing and developmentally supportive."
Moore[5]

Once again it is noteworthy that this aspect occurs frequently in other research conducted with children. Robin Moore found that children's feelings about the 'hurtful' asphalt environment was supported by accidents records kept by the school; these showed that many so-called accidents could be attributed to the nature of the design of the physical environment. Moore notes in terms of the development of the Washington Schoolyard, that incidents and accidents reduced the day that the development work began.

One of the most frequent comments by teachers in our research related to the problems experienced with children when they had been in the grounds on a windy day. There is a widely held belief that this meteorological phenomenon causes virtual hyperactivity in some children and seems to affect the majority by making them more boisterous than usual. Many school sites are situated in exposed locations and school grounds do seem to be exceptionally cold and windy places. Yet in the majority of cases such environments provide no form of shelter or indeed shade from the sun (which in one school visited was sufficiently strong to soften the tarmac!) - or even planting to act as a wind break.

The lack of built shelters is all the more surprising given our climate and the universal hatred of 'wet playtimes' by children and adults alike. Shelters were once a common feature of school design and, where they still remain, are highly prized.

Whilst children in our research rarely commented on the need for seats many children talked of the lack of "places to be" with one or two special friends, or of places to sit to play games, tell stories or read a book. This suggests that the provision of seating should be related to the creation of social spaces where seating facilitates opportunities for interaction and engagement with others, rather than seats and benches for the sake of them.

As Robin Moore asserts, environmental quality is an "extremely fuzzy concept, especially when applied to intimate human spaces... residing neither in person nor in environment, but in an evolving relationship between them". Whilst it would require a comprehensive design guide to address all the facets which need to be considered to address this issue effectively, one way of approaching the problem is to ask, as a child did in our research, "Would you come here if you didn't have to?".

3.5 THE IMPORTANCE OF DIVERSITY, VARIETY AND MANIPULATION

In our research a key factor to the successful design of school grounds related to the extent to which they offered diversity and were manipulable by the children. This finding is consistent with all other research we could find relating to both school and non school environments used by children.

For this reason, elements of school grounds which were 'natural' were regularly identified as having special significance for the children, from the leaves which trees 'gave them' to roll and hide in, to the fact that the natural environment provided lots of interesting things to study and explore and "really look at".

"Environmental diversity banishes boredom, supports the development of each child's personality and skills and provides essential opportunities for learning through playful exploration and manipulation of one's surroundings."
Moore[5]

Moore constantly re-iterates the importance of providing natural resource settings, having found in all his research that natural elements are most favoured by children.

Many eminent researchers have investigated the phenomena of "the ambiguous, hidden, wild, unkempt, leftover places of childhood days"[9] and generally find that the diversity and manipulability afforded by such places are the primary reason for their enduring attraction.

The concept of 'affordances' was developed by Gibson[10] who asserts that affordances are features of the environment which are identified because of their functional significance for the person in the environment; thus a tree 'affords' climbing, vegetation 'affords' hiding.

One example of the way in which a diverse natural setting affords children's experience and opportunity relates to their need for privacy. In our research, places which provided opportunity for hiding were highly prized. Thus, whilst bushes were "boring" they were valued because they afforded opportunity for hiding.

In 'Nature as refuge in children's environments'[11], Mary Ann Kirkby explores the significance of 'refuges' for children and reports on research undertaken to compare the use of different types of refuges in playgrounds used by children. Kirkby used a timed behavioural mapping technique and found that 47% of play use occurred in three different types of refuge, which took up only 10% of the total play area.

In our research, children constantly bemoaned the lack of refuges, describing the many roles and functions these provide. Children clearly enjoyed the fun of hiding from others (friends and adults!) but refuges often held greater significance. The ability to find a private place in a public space held great importance and significance for the children, offering them peace and quiet but also somewhere to get away from others. The value of nooks and crannies to children in school environments has been recorded by various researchers.

Whilst many concerned about incidence of bullying in school grounds advocate removal or restriction of access to bushes, dens or nooks and crannies, research suggests that, certainly for younger children, the opportunity to find refuge in the school grounds may play an important part in reducing such problems.

3.6 THE PROVISION OF FIXED PLAY EQUIPMENT

Diversity and the ability to manipulate environments has been shown to be of considerable importance in terms of the provision of equipment and materials for play. Research relating to fixed play equipment has indicated for many years that the most successful is that which enables children to manipulate and change its form and use. In our research this was undoubtedly proven, given the preferences of children for smaller elements which can be changed either in a real sense or at least in their imagination.

Whilst the majority of research data available relating to fixed play equipment is drawn from non-school settings, it provides a valuable source of information which should be carefully considered before such items are introduced into school grounds. For example, research conducted in Sweden, reported in *The Impossible Playground*[13], compares the use of play equipment on different types of playgrounds and shows that in relation to the total time spent on the playgrounds, very little involved use of equipment.

"Nearly half of the equipment was used for less than 2% of the time children were on the playground. Other equipment had an average use rate of 3 - 5%. Even play equipment which was well used was not in use for more than 15 - 20% of the total playtime."
Noren-Bjorn[13]

This and other research which has produced similar findings has particular significance for schools because children are likely to spend much more time, more regularly, in the grounds than on an out-of-school playground. The majority of such equipment may not have been designed originally for use in school grounds and its 'sustainability' in terms of children's interest should be carefully considered. Another important factor involves the quantity of equipment in relation to the likely number of users which, in school grounds, is again likely to be greater, at any one time, that in non-school situations.

All fixed play equipment for use outdoors should conform to current guidelines and standards which take account of age appropriateness, location, the need for special surfacing in some cases, maintenance and inspection requirements etc. Schools should consult the Health and Safety Officer of their Local Education Authority before taking any decisions regarding the provision of fixed play equipment in school grounds.

Fixed play equipment usually serves a range of basic functions for children at play, such as climbing, swinging, sliding etc. Whilst opportunities to undertake such activities are valuable for children, physical activities serve to meet only an element of children's play needs and such items should not be expected to provide a 'panacea' in an otherwise sterile environment.

3.7 THE IMPORTANCE OF PARTICIPATION AND INVOLVEMENT BY CHILDREN

"The participatory design process is essential to the over-arching goal of making school sites an environmental amenity rather than a teaching factory." Eriksen

Scrutiny of research relating to the design of school grounds consistently points to the importance of involving children to achieve 'good' outcomes. The concept of participation in relation to management policy and practice is explored in the next chapter of this Section. In reality, it is likely that where the concept of participation by children is practised in schools, this will be a fully integrated concept. We have already drawn attention to the problems of separating elements of the discussion in this document, which has been necessary purely for ease of presentation. On the subject of participation by children, this point merits emphasis because experience would suggest that an ad-hoc or piece-meal approach to this matter may prove counter-productive.

"The adult is not usually capable of experiencing what the child experiences, more often than not, he is not even capable of imagining what the child experiences. It would not be surprising, then, that he should be incapable of recalling his own childhood experiences since his whole mode of experiencing has changed." Schachtel[14]

There can be little doubt that where children are consulted, appropriately, about the design of provision for them, a better understanding of their needs is achieved and design outcomes are usually more successful.

School grounds design

The extent to which adults find it difficult to design 'ideal' environments for children is demonstrated by research conducted by Bishop, Peterson and Michaels[15] who used a new design consultation methodology to establish children's preferences in terms of play environments. The same methodology was used with a group of administrators and designers who were asked to make choices as if they were eight year olds. The researchers found that there was little correlation between the children's choices and those of the adults, and conclude that most adults are incapable of accurately predicting children's preferences.

Some schools in our research had undertaken school grounds development projects. In some cases children had been consulted about proposals, in others they had not and the differences became quite clear from the views of the children themselves.

It was particularly interesting that many schools which had involved children commented on the fact that they often suggested quite simple - and relatively cheap - ways to improve the design of the grounds. However, the process of consultation, the way the exercise is conducted and presented to the children, will have considerable influence on the outcome.

For example, where children are asked what they would like to *do* in the grounds, a wide and diverse range of activities and experiences will usually result. Where they are asked what they would like to *have*, swimming pools and Disney World type schemes are likely to feature on everyone's list! Clearly, for children there is a big difference between 'having' and 'doing'.

However, where participation is extended to enable active involvement and participation in change and in caring for the grounds, the most beneficial results have been recorded. From our research the active involvement of children constantly emerged as a critical factor influencing their behaviour and also their attitude, not only in terms of the grounds, but in relation to themselves and the school as a whole.

"The trouble is they put things in funny places. Like the benches. They put them where we play football so you can't sit there. If you're playing relay or rounders with your class you have to mind the benches or you trip over when you try to catch the ball. There are benches everywhere, so you can't really play."

"You must make the kids realise that you are not interested in just being pleased... you have to be very careful and it is a difficult art to elicit something from children which is apart from what they think you, an adult, might want." Kerns[8]

"Children felt a sense of importance and of being especially chosen for their talents. Every child here has actually done something within this playground - and that's great. They can really call it their playground. That's what it is." Kerns[8]

"The trouble is there's nothing to do and anyway they put the flowers in the wrong places where you can't help but trample on them and then it's a complete waste of money."

In our research, children were keen to be involved with the grounds, to play their part in improving and maintaining them. Moreover, where children had been involved, they were adamant that their participation was critical to the way they felt about the results.

Our review of research identified a considerable number of case studies of school grounds developments involving children from Canada, Australia, America, Finland, France, Germany, Sweden and other countries. It is interesting to note the consistency with which these reports highlight the wide range of benefits which result from children's participation in such initiatives. Most lay great emphasis on the significance of the process.

Changes in children's attitude and behaviour most commonly mentioned include heightened self esteem; a reduction in aggression, accidents and incidents of damage and vandalism; improved morale; reduction in truancy levels, and generally a change in the atmosphere of the whole school. Reports of increased parental and community support are also common.

3.8 THE RELATIONSHIP BETWEEN DESIGN AND DAMAGE

A further link between the design of school grounds and children's behaviour may be found by considering the issue of damage. During our research, children often drew attention to places where damage frequently occured, but which they felt to be unavoidable.

The distinction between different types of damage which occurs on school sites is well explained in a paper by John Zeisel, Architecture and Research Officer, Harvard Graduate School of Design[16]. This paper reports on a survey conducted to investigate the way pupils used schools in order to improve their design. By analysing the types of property damage according to the motive of the person being destructive and the indirect effect, Zeisel identifies four categories; Malicious Vandalism; Misnamed Vandalism; Non-Malicious Property Damage; Hidden Maintenance Damage.

School grounds design

Zeisel points out that (in America) malicious vandalism causes under fifty per cent of school property damage, yet designers and planners have primarily directed their attention towards defending schools against this form of damage.

Zeisel's research concentrated on the other fifty per cent in an attempt to identify design and management solutions. One of the key points raised in the report relates to the fact that much of the damage found in schools was caused by lack of recognition of the need to plan and design for the informal and social needs of the users, as well as for formal educational needs.

Another major finding was that the design of school environments sometimes challenges young people to overcome design faults by attempting to find their own solutions. He suggests that those who plan and design school environments must "take at least some responsibility for design decisions which challenge young people to damage schools and which make schools easy targets". Zeisels team visited and studied schools across the USA and analysed the nature of property damage and the causes. His findings present some fascinating solutions to many problems commonly experienced in UK schools.

What is of particular interest here is the recognition that the design and nature of schools (buildings and grounds) actually contributes to and causes problems in terms of damage and vandalism, not only by the very nature of the design but also because of the messages and meanings which design conveys to the users.

"If a child needs to cross a river but does not know how to swim, there are several ways to deal with the problem. The first is to build a high fence on the river's edge to keep the child away. Depending on the child's need to cross the river, and depending on how much he is challenged by the fence itself, he may climb it, break it down or cut through it, and eventually drown anyway. On the other hand, if a bridge is built to the other side, the child can achieve his own goals safely and without doing harm to any property. We are concentrating our efforts to find solutions which act as bridges to meet the needs of school users, rather than those which act as challenging fences." Zeisel[16]

113

References from section three, chapter three

(1)   Aaron, D. and Winawer, B. ◆ *Child's Play: A Creative Approach to Playscapes for Today's Children* ◆ 1965 ◆ Harper & Row.

(2)   Gump, P. V. ◆ 'Ecological Psychology and Issues of Play' ◆ In *The Ecological Context of Children's Play* ◆ Bloch and Pellegrini (Eds) ◆ Abley Publishing Corporation.

(3)   Carpenter, C. J., Huston, A., Spera, L. ◆ 'Children's Use of Time in Their Everyday Activities During Middle Childhood' ◆ In *The Ecological Context of Children's Play* ◆ Bloch and Pellegrini (Eds) ◆ Abley Publishing Corporation.

(4)   Rothenberg, M., Hayward, D. G., Beasley, R. ◆ 'Playgrounds: For Whom?' ◆ In *Man-Environment Interactions - Part 111*, EDRA 5 ◆ Carson, D.H. (Ed) ◆ 1974 ◆ Dowden, Hutchinson & Ross.

(5)   Moore, Robin ◆ 'Before and After Asphalt: Diversity as an Ecological Measure of Quality in Children's Outdoor Environments' ◆ In *The Ecological Context of Children's Play* ◆ Bloch and Pellegrini (Eds) ◆ Abley Publishing Corporation.

(6)   Moore, Robin ◆ 'Generating Relevant Urban Childhood Places: Learning from the Yard'.◆ In *Innovations in Play Environments* ◆ Wilkinson, P. (Ed) ◆ 1980 ◆ Croom Helm ◆ ISBN 0 7099 0024 4.

(7)   Christie, J. and Johnsen E. P. ◆ 'The Constraints of Settings on Children's Play' ◆ In *Play and Culture Vol.2 No.4* ◆ November 1989.

(8)   Kerns, A. ◆ 'The Story of A Playground: Study of St. Mary's School, Erskinville' ◆ In *Architecture Australia No.68.*

(9)   Lukashok, A. and Lynch, K. ◆ 'Some childhood memories of the city' ◆ In *Journal of the American Institute of Planners* ◆ 1956.

(10)   Gibson, J. J. ◆ *The Ecological Approach to Visual Perception* ◆ 1966 ◆ Houghton Mifflin.

(11)   Kirkby, MaryAnn ◆ 'Nature as refuge in children's environments' ◆ In *CEQ Vol.6 No.1 Children and Vegetation* ◆ Spring 1989 ◆ Children's Environments Research Group, The City University of New York ◆ ISSN 0886 0505.

(12)   Ward, Colin ◆ *The Child in the City* ◆ 1977 ◆ Architectural Press, London ◆ ISBN 0 85139 118 4.

(13)   Noren-Bjorn, Eva ◆ *The Impossible Playground* ◆ 1982 ◆ Leisure Press ◆ ISBN 0 918438 88 8.

(14)   Schachtel, E. ◆ 'On Memory and Childhood Amnesia' ◆ In *Journal of the Biology and Pathology of Interpersonal Relations Vol.10* ◆ 1947.

(15)   Bishop, R.L., Peterson, G.L., Michaels, R.M. ◆ 'Measurement of children's preferences for the play environment' ◆ In *Environmental Design, Research and Practice* ◆ Mitchell, W.J. (Ed) ◆ 1972 ◆ Dowden, Hutchinson & Ross.

(16)   Zeisel, J. ◆ 'Designing out unintentional school property damage: A checklist' ◆ In *Man-Environment Interactions - Part 111*, EDRA 5 ◆ Carson, D. H. (Ed) ◆ 1974 ◆ Dowden, Hutchinson & Ross.

CHAPTER FOUR
Children's attitude and behaviour are influenced by the way the school grounds are managed

"Play is to a child work, thought, art and relaxation and cannot be pressed into any single formula. It expresses a child's relation to himself and his environment and, without adequate opportunity for play, normal and satisfactory emotional development is not possible."
Margaret Lowenfield

This Chapter explores the following issues:

◆ Management of the Informal Currriculum and the organisation of playtime.

◆ The purpose of the Informal Curriculum.

◆ The role of dinner time supervisors.

◆ The use of loose equipment.

◆ Some further aspects relating to management policy and practice.

◆ Some alternative management stategies.

◆ Maintenance.

It also contains:

◆ Suggested Activities.

◆ References.

4 Children's attitude and behaviour are influenced by the way the school grounds are managed

4.1 INTRODUCTION

The range of ways in which management policy and practice influences children's attitudes and behaviour are many, varied and essentially interrelated. This includes the way the grounds, as physical environments, are maintained and cared for; the way children's use of them for the Informal Curriculum is organised and managed; whether the grounds are used for extra-curricular purposes; whether the grounds provide an amenity for the general public, and whether they are used by the school for the Formal Curriculum.

Our research suggests that children read signs and symbols from the way school grounds are managed which sets up a cultural framework which significantly influences their attitude and behaviour. Thus management practice and policy in relation to the grounds as a whole constitutes an important and influential element of the Hidden Curriculum of school grounds.

Chapter Two of this section explored the way the grounds signify the values and intentions of the school as a whole. The previous chapter dealt with the relationship between the physical design of the grounds and children's behaviour, and identified clear connections between the quality of the environment and the quality of children's experience in using it.

There are, however, certain aspects relating to the management of the grounds which we found to be especially influential in terms of children's attitudes and behaviour and which need to be addressed separately in some detail. This chapter therefore deals with the management of the Informal Curriculum and maintenance of the grounds in general.

4.2   MANAGEMENT OF THE INFORMAL CURRICULUM

The management of play and playtime – the Informal Curriculum – has become an issue of particular concern for many schools and therefore formed a substantial part of the research project. During the past couple of years, a great deal of material has been generated by those concerned about 'problems' arising during or as a result of playtime. In the majority of cases this material focuses on managing children's behaviour and presents strategies for behaviour modification, often in isolation from the influence exerted by the design of the physical environment.

"It is ridiculous to teach children to lead creative lives in the classroom if we turn them into a playground where all they have to do is fight and fall down."
Anon

Whilst almost any material which recognises the need to improve children's play opportunities in schools is generally to be welcomed, our research suggests that unless due account is taken of the effect of the environment on children's behaviour, the root cause of many of the problems will not be recognised and any strategies to modify children's behaviour are likely to be, at best, only partially successful. A great deal of research exists which indicates that, where the physical environment has been improved and change occurs in terms of children's behaviour, the cause lies as much in the process of change as in the outcome. In addition, many of the schools throughout the country which have embarked on changes to their school grounds testify to this fact. This would suggest that in the process, changes are wrought in management practice and policy which, in themselves, are very significant, and that in order to fully understand the cause and nature of change it is necessary to consider all aspects of management policy and practice.

Whilst the effect of the design of the place where children play on the way they behave cannot be over-emphasised, the potential of even the most wonderful environment can be diminished by rules which restrict the way it can be used and, conversely, well managed playtimes can greatly extend the potential of quite barren and uninspiring grounds.

THE ORGANISATION OF PLAYTIME

From our research and other studies, the organisation of playtime in primary schools varies considerably. Some schools have maintained the tradition of three break times: mid-morning, lunchtime and mid-afternoon . However, there is evidence of a shift towards removing the mid afternoon break. Others operate flexible playtimes during the morning and afternoon where teachers decide when to take a break, according to the programme of work each day. This seems most common in small schools.

The length of time devoted to the Informal Curriculum also varies. In some cases, particularly with infants, the lunchtime break may extend to an hour and a half, though most commonly it is about an hour. Taken overall, therefore, the Informal Curriculum can account for anything between 25% and 33% of the school day.

4.3 THE PURPOSE OF THE INFORMAL CURRICULUM

Whilst it has been stated elsewhere that it is not the intention of this document to deal in detail with the subject of play, it is important that schools consider the purpose and value of the Informal Curriculum. Reference has already been made to a selection of work which considers aspects of play and its value generally and further details are included in Section Four.

Play is a complex phenomenon. Through playing children learn what they cannot be taught. Play is essentially intrinsically motivated and self-directed, but that does not mean it is aimless, purposeless or merely about 'letting off steam'. Opportunities to play are important to children's physical, social and intellectual development; to their health and well-being both during childhood and throughout adult life. It has long been recognised that children who lack opportunity to play may fail to develop a range of essential human skills, and that this can lead to problems for them as individuals and for the adults who care for and teach them.

We have already drawn attention to the fact that play in school, in terms of the Informal Curriculum (i.e. play and playtime, as opposed to play as part of the Formal Curriculum), has received relatively little attention in terms of research. Examination of that which does exist indicates that the Informal Curriculum is different in many ways from play in other settings for a variety of reasons, which have implications in terms of both the design and management of school grounds.

In an article entitled 'School Playground as Festival'[1], Brian Sutton-Smith draws on his own work and others, particularly that of Eifermann, in order to identify the special cultural significance of playtime in schools. Eifermann conducted a study in the 1960s in dozens of school playgrounds in Israel, involving over 100,000 children, which yielded a wealth of information about the culture of school playground activities[2].

"We can sum up by saying there is a culture of school playground play, just as there is a culture of schooling, of sporting organisations, and of mothers' clubs. Further the school-playground child culture is apparently one of the most important as far as the children are concerned, at least as judged by their most frequent choice of 'recess' as their favourite school subject and their continued identification of such play opportunities with the establishment of peer friendships." Sutton-Smith[1]

Amongst many conclusions Sutton-Smith draws, he is particularly concerned to highlight the cultural uniqueness of playtime in school and the many benefits this offers to both individual children and in terms of childhood generally. He further argues that this opportunity is of such importance that the growing trend in America towards reduction and even abolition of 'recess' time represents a basic contravention of children's rights.

The dearth of research which exists relating to playtime may have contributed to the relative absence of discussion or definition of the purpose and value of the Informal Curriculum. Despite the fact that the Informal Curriculum provides essential learning opportunities for children and accounts for such a substantial part of every child's school life, our research indicates that schools rarely produce any form of clarification or statement about what it is for and why it exists. This lack of recognition can lead to a devaluation of the Informal Curriculum, of the place where it takes place and of the people who manage it. The absence of clarification of the purpose and value of the Informal Curriculum amongst pupils, teachers, supervisors and parents, has been seen to lead to assumption and confusion in terms of management policy and practice. It may also result in playtime being a less than positive and enjoyable learning experience for everyone concerned.

4.4   THE ROLE OF DINNER TIME SUPERVISORS

In the majority of primary schools in England and Wales, supervision of morning and afternoon playtime is undertaken by teachers and mid-day playtime by Dinner Time Supervisors (DTSs).

Without a clear understanding of the purpose and value of the Informal Curriculum, it may be difficult to define the role and function of those whose job it is to supervise children at this time.

During the first phase of research undertaken by LTL, a questionnaire was circulated to a representative sample of Education Authorities asking for copies of job descriptions and contracts of employment for DTSs. From the material returned there was little concensus about what the job involved and, in many cases, examples included tasks which were either inappropriate or quite impossible. For example "chasing and competitive games should not be allowed" and "play on outdoor equipment should always be orderly and disciplined". At the time, many authorities could not supply any information.

Whilst teachers often freely admit that 'doing playground duty' is not one of their favourite tasks, their training and skill, familiarity with the children and ability to impose sanctions when necessary, may make the lack of clarification less important for them. However, in our experience, the situation is very different for DTSs.

In Australia, all playtime is supervised by teachers. Research conducted by John Evans of Deakin University[3] amongst 120 primary school teachers investigated the job of the playtime supervisor. Teachers recorded separate elements of the role as being a police officer; referee; confidante; counsellor and player, with the most common roles involving arbitration and first aid skills. Not surprisingly, the majority disliked playground duty! One main finding from the study was that teachers felt they were inadequately prepared for the role and responsibilities of being playground supervisors because this required a range of

"We would never consider allowing an unqualified person to teach in the classroom, yet we care little about the knowledge or nature of the person who supervises the playground."
Evans[3]

different skills to that of teaching. They also noted the need for training about the value of play in primary schools in general.

Evans also found that in restricted, less stimulating environments, teachers reported more interpersonal conflict, fighting and the need for greater intervention. Where the playground offered space, a variety of equipment and surfaces, and where rules allowed freedom to play, teachers had fewer problems to contend with.

As part of our research, a pilot training course for headteachers and dinner time supervisors was trialled. This involved headteachers or teachers from more than 50 schools and almost 250 supervisors. The DTSs identified a variety of issues and concerns, amongst the most common being their lack of status and a feeling of being devalued by children, parents and staff.

Other purely practical considerations arose and clearly need review. For example, in some schools supervisors are expected to work with a ratio of one to 60 and even 75 children. This is clearly unreasonable and relegates the role of supervisors to that of simply patrolling or policing.

Children involved in our research were very conscious of the status of dinner time supervisors within the hierarchy of their school. The fact that such staff were often unable to exercise any real authority was well understood and sometimes manipulated by children. Other meaningful symbols for them included the fact that DTSs often wore overalls when doing playground duty but teachers never did!

In a number of schools where DTSs were also employed as classroom assistants, the headteachers and the DTSs themselves noted that this changed the nature of their relationship with the children, parents and other staff.

The connection between the role of supervisors and children's behaviour is most interesting. Many of the studies we found which explore the behaviour of children at playtime suggest that if supervisors are prepared sometimes to engage with children in their play (as opposed to organising them) their behaviour improves. There are of course additional factors to

Some of the most common problems raised by dinner time supervisors:
- *lack of status*
- *lack of respect*
- *lack of expertise/training*
- *lack of equipment*
- *insufficient ratio of supervisors to children*
- *lack of involvement in other aspects of school management/ poor communication with teaching staff*
- *inability to deal with behaviour problems*
- *the nature of the environment.*

"At playtime someone needs to make sure things are protected, if the little ones do something wrong they need to be told. The dinner ladies don't care, they see a child trampling but they say it doesn't matter and let him carry on but then they can't do anything anyway."

consider here and it is most important to stress that it is all too easy to 'tip the balance' from being an adult who can engage with children from time to time, to one who attempts to structure and organise them in such a way that the nature of the activity itself it changed.

This is clearly identifed in a study conducted by Van der Kooij[4] which set out to identify the relationship between play and behavioural disorders. The author suggests that children's lack of ability (opportunity) to play with adults may be a cause of certain behavioural disorders, and that it is striking that educators and children are not playing together any longer. He notes the increasing use of play therapy, which often produces "a kind of miracle medicine in the fight against inadequate behaviour" but suggests that "prevention is better than therapy".

Whilst it would be unreasonable and inappropriate to suggest that supervisors should spend their entire time playing with children, the evidence that a degree of sensitive and infrequent involvement improves the experience is worth consideration, not only in terms of the children but because it is likely to enhance the role for the adults involved.

In one school, which has a relatively impoverished site, the headteacher organised a programme of teaching children traditional games and made a point of being in the grounds at playtime. She believes that this produced a range of beneficial outcomes and, interestingly, her own involvement was much commented upon and appreciated by her pupils.

The role and value of traditional games as a part of children's play is a subject of study in its own right! Many schools report great benefit from the introduction of both traditional and co-operative games as part of the Formal Curriculum on the quality of children's play and behaviour generally. Apart from the intrinsic value this can have in increasing children's repertoire of games, it is interesting to consider that much of the value may derive from the (albeit initial) involvement of adults. Perhaps this fact alone alters the 'cultural status' of the activity.

"From my clinical experience I know that playing together can have the function of prevention as well as therapeutic influence upon threatening or already manifest distrubances. The effect often will be a reorientation in the pedagogical relations." Van der Kooij[4]

"The games have worked because adult involvement has added dignity to what the children are doing, it's not the game itself that's important but the fact that an adult has taken the trouble to get involved which changes things." Mrs. K. Samuels, Head, St. Jude's School, Manchester

"Our headteacher skips so if you've got nothing to do you can play with her. She's always there and she sees everything."

A study conducted in schools in New Zealand by Maris O'Rourke[5], compared the behaviour of children in a school playground before and after the introduction of what she calls 'supplies'. O'Rourke introduced moveable equipment and playleaders into the playground and found that the incidence of severe aggression was reduced to less than half the baseline rate. She found that under all conditions, large numbers of children played, very few children broke any rules and there was no fighting. She also found a correlation between the level of adult participation and children's involvement in activities.

A similar study conducted by the Swedish Child Council[6] involved playleaders from the Parks Department working with children during playtime in schools. Amongst the many interesting findings in this study, the authors note that the introduction of personnel trained to work with children in play settings had great impact, particularly in schools with pupils of many different nationalities where conflict and other problems were greatest.

This study further describes a school with serious vandalism problems where the workers introduced loose equipment and children were made responsible for looking after the materials. The project was so successful that it was extended.

From the above it would appear that whilst the introduction of equipment and games to school playgrounds has a wide range of benefits, the involvement and the role of adults was a central and very significant factor in the success of the experiments.

4.5   THE USE OF LOOSE EQUIPMENT

This evidence led us to investigate the extent of use of loose equipment in UK schools as part of the Informal Curriculum. It quickly became clear that the matter of loose equipment – to have or not to have – was an issue about which opinions varied greatly. Many schools expressed concern that this would increase incidence of squabbling and fighting, that the materials would all be lost or stolen and that generally it would make matters worse not better.

However, we could find no authoritative research conducted in the UK on the subject and as a result, a small study was commissioned from Hull University as part of our research project. Quantities of equipment were introduced into six primary schools and the effect was monitored. The equipment, which was provided free of charge by NES Arnold, was selected to provide a non-specific range of items, including a variety of balls, quoits, hoops, beanbags, small cones, chalk and skipping ropes.

Overall, the equipment was found to improve playtime and, in the majority of cases, schools reported a variety of additional benefits from the experiment. One school experienced problems and the study was therefore discontinued early.

In addition to the specific issue under investigation, the study highlighted some critical factors related to the management of playtime generally and to the role of supervisors in particular. For example, those schools which involved children in the management of the equipment reported the widest range of benefits from the experiment.

The reaction of teaching and non-teaching staff to the experiment was markedly different in some schools and these were notably the schools where problems arose – not in terms of the use of equipment by children – but in terms of the way the adults managed and organised the scheme.

A number of important considerations emerged from the research which are probably integral to the success of the introduction of loose equipment generally. First, there needs to be a sufficient quantity of equipment in relation to the number of children who may wish to use it. This doesn't mean that every child should have his/her own ball to play with: on the other hand, one ball amongst two hundred children is very likely to cause arguments! Secondly, the equipment will probably get very heavy use. It should therefore be reasonably durable and of good quality but inevitably, as with all consumable supplies, it will suffer wear and tear and provision needs to be made for the replenishment of the stock. Thirdly, if the equipment can be changed from time to time, perhaps on a termly basis, children's interest in it will sustain for longer.

The LTL study into the introduction of loose equipment showed:
- *children enjoyed the equipment*
- *it increased activity levels and use of space*
- *it increased the range and variety of play*
- *it did not cause any increase in accidents or incidents*
- *some schools reported a decrease in accidents and/or incidents of aggression*
- *schools reported an increase in sharing, co-operation and interaction amongst children.*

"They gave us a box of things for lunchtime but it was just a load of torn-up magazines and games with bits missing."

123

4.6 SOME FURTHER ASPECTS RELATING TO MANAGEMENT POLICY AND PRACTICE

In analysing data collected during our research it is noticeable how frequently children reported that they were "not allowed" to do various things related to the grounds. Whilst the need for rules and regulations in the management of the grounds and the children is beyond doubt, it is interesting to note two common factors which emerged from analysis of our data. First, children often appeared puzzled over certain rules which were imposed and secondly, rather than alleviate problems, sometimes these rules actually appeared to exacerbate the situation.

"We've got a lot of grass but we can't use it ever. Teachers don't let us go on it 'cos they say we'll make a mess."

"It would be good if we could go on the grass sometimes but they won't let us near it when it's wet and it's always wet, even when it's dry."

One example which frequently arose relates to the use of grass. In some cases, whilst the grounds overall provided sufficient space for children at playtime, grassed areas were put 'out-of-bounds' for a substantial part of the year with the result that children were able to use only a relatively small area of tarmac. It was common in such cases to find that staff were concerned about aggression and fighting and a high level of 'incidents' generally during playtime. There are of course many good reasons why such a rule might need to be imposed. However, the level of problems caused by a large number of children trying to play on too small a space merits careful review of such restrictions.

There are of course many cases where the school site is severely restricted and where the situation is governed by physical constraints rather than management policy. However, in other cases, careful re-appraisal and reconsideration has led schools to identify various ways of overcoming such problems.

Some schools have extended the use of grassed areas for the Informal Curriculum by requiring that children wear wellington boots if the grass is wet or damp. This takes a degree of organisation and space is required to store the boots, but this can be less hassle than having all the children playing on a small tarmacced area. Apparently parents are usually only too willing to donate boots to a 'general welly fund'.

School grounds management

We found that many of the rules employed by supervisors in an attempt to restrict usage of the grounds had been instituted because they felt it necessary to be able to see all of the children at all times. In some cases, where schools have no secure boundary fence, this was a source of great concern. In others where this was not the case, the rule was sometimes borne of the fact that the ratio of supervisors to children was too low.

For children, the fact that many parts of the grounds which they found interesting were the ones to which access was restricted was a source of considerable frustration, particularly where the rest of the space provided little stimulation and opportunity. Equally, when children did not fully understand the reasons for the rules, this created a permanent source of tension and conflict, and some children used the rule as the basis for 'games' which merely tested the patience and endurance of the adults involved.

Another rule, commonly imposed in school grounds, involves zoning of space in order to segregate children by age. In some schools the size of the school roll made separate dinner times and therefore playtimes a necessity. But in others children shared the same playtime but were not allowed to play together. This rule was sometimes created out of fear that young children would be injured by the boisterous play of older ones or was merely a tradition that no-one had questioned.

In our research, junior age children (both boys and girls) often expressed regret about this rule where it was imposed and it was interesting that, in those schools where children were allowed to mix freely, they were often seen to do so.

Concern for children's safety is obviously an important consideration. However, zoning space by activity rather than age has helped some schools address such concerns whilst maintaining opportunities for children to mix .

Whilst some rules are obviously essential and each school site, being unique, will present its own problems, the way in which rules are made, conveyed and enforced has been found to be a critical factor in terms of children's attitudes and behaviour.

4.7 SOME ALTERNATIVE MANAGEMENT STRATEGIES

As discussed in Chapter Two of this Section, evidence exists that increased involvement and participation of children has been shown to yield many benefits in terms of children's attitude and behaviour generally.

One aspect which arose during our research and which has implications in terms of management, is the concept of schools (or pupils) councils and the establishment of 'Playground Codes'. Many schools which have instituted the concept of schools councils report that the benefits can be considerable and wide ranging. In his book *Playtime in the Primary School*[7], Peter Blatchford discusses the benefits of a schools council as experienced in one junior school in inner London where it was found that children felt more confident about handling playground disputes; it encouraged children to think realistically about the consequences of decisions and it had developed a moral dimension to the children's contributions.

The nature and form of schools councils may vary considerably from school to school. However it seems that the key to their success lies in the fact that their very existence changes some fundamental aspects of school management policy and it is possibly these changes which in themselves bring benefit.

From our research it is clear that some children believe that some adults fail to take account of those things which matter to children; that they do not always listen when children talk about things which matter to them, particularly if the adults deem these to be unimportant. Whilst schools councils provide opportunity for children to raise all kinds of issues, from experience, play and playtime will often form a substantial part of their considerations. The existence of a channel through which children's views and feelings about play and playtime and other aspects of school life can be discussed and considered with the teaching staff will inevitably increase their understanding of children's perspectives which, in itself, must surely bring benefits.

However, it is also possible that the real benefit lies in the fact that the very existence of this channel of communication, in itself, raises the status of the Informal Curriculum by demonstrating to the children that this aspect of school life is recognised as having value and importance to those who manage the school.

The real as well as the symbolic significance of strategies designed to increase children's participation and involvement was explored in detail by Pia Bjorklid, who conducted research into pupil participation funded by the Department of Educational Research in Sweden in 1985[8]. Bjorklid explains that, in Sweden, the National Curriculum states: "The school has an obligation to give pupils increased responsibility and powers of influence in line with their increasing maturity and age." Many schools implement this requirement by the establishement of class committees or councils. Bjorklid's research set out to examine the extent of joint influence of primary school children in the control and shaping of their school environment.

Bjorklid finds that in the schools studied, the concept of responsibility related mainly to chores such as cleaning up after others and being head of table at lunchtime. The teachers believed that such chores partly helped to lighten their own workload but also provided a more pleasant working environment. However, the children considered that most of the jobs were boring, particularly those which infringed breaktimes. The only positive responses related to tasks which involved caring for pets or flowers. These were considered "hard work" but attractive.

Whilst many children expressed a desire to discuss and participate in the resolution of problems such as conflicts relating to social behaviour, this was usually prohibited because teachers felt the structure to be inappropriate.

Bjorklid concludes that whilst discussion of individual and personal conflict situations may not have been feasible, the general concepts behind questions of discipline and conduct could and should be included in such forums. She suggests that children must be allowed to be more actively involved in

"The point I wish to make is that for those decisions one cannot influence or help to make, one can feel no great personal responsibility.

In order to be able to act from an adequate level of moral understanding and thereby exert real influence, a mutuality or reciprocity of relations among children, and between children and adults, is important. This does not of course mean that teachers should abdicate their responsibility, only that they should respect the children's competance and listen to them."

decisions relating to their own environments because they are most directly affected and more qualified to make assessments, and that schools have an important role to play in enabling involvement and participation. However, she states that this requires a fundamental change by adults towards a "relationship of reciprocal change" if pseudo-democracy and tokensim is not to be the result.

4.8   MAINTENANCE

In our research children very were conscious of the condition of the grounds and the way these were maintained. Because children spent a great deal of time in the grounds and were generally intimately familiar with the place, they noticed even the smallest detail.

"The first thing I think about outside is the rubbish around, it's everywhere and there's all paint sprayed on the walls and lots of litter and it's terrible because of the mess."

A great deal of research exists which suggests that if children are provided with an environment which is cared for and maintained to a good standard, the majority, at least, will adopt that standard. Certainly those familiar with the habits of children will recognise the tendency for them to put their finger in a small hole and make it bigger! There is undoubtedly a difference between this behaviour and wilful vandalism as there is between damage caused to the school by its own pupils as opposed to other people. The issue of vandalism perpetrated outside school time is without the remit of this study, though certain aspects and results of such problems were sigificant in our study and are obviously of major concern to schools.

"A dilapidated appearance can evoke an uncaring attitude... accidental damage, even if minor, may lead to damage appearing elsewhere." DES[9]

A paper published by the DES, *Vandalism in schools and colleges - - some possible ways of reducing damage*[9], explores many of the issues and provides some positive suggestions which have been shown to reduce problems in terms of school sites. Whilst the report suggests that the overall design and quality of the environment is important, it also recognises the need for keeping premises in good repair. The report suggests other preventative measures including greater involvement of pupils and the community at large, and extended out of hours use.

School grounds management

Where schools suffer badly from litter/debris and evidence of damage caused out of school hours, it is obviously difficult to ensure that the effects and evidence are always speedily removed. However, apart from the potential health hazard such material may pose, from our research it is clear that these kinds of problems have a considerable affect on pupils.

During our research children expressed anger and frustration where the school had been vandalised, and were often puzzled by what they perceived to be an appararent lack of determination on the part of the school to find and punish the perpetrators. Where children had been involved in developing or caring for the grounds, their reaction to acts of vandalism was significantly heightened and the matter became a very personal one.

Various studies indicate that where management practices have been changed, in terms of both the maintenance of the grounds and the management of children using them, this often appears to result in a decrease in vandalism.

The value of involvement and participation by children has already been dealt with in some detail in other sections. However, it is worth noting here that this has been found to yield positive benefits in terms of the maintenance of the physical environment as well as on the attitudes of pupils.

"It's not only the kids that do damage but we always get the blame... we found cigarette butts in our flower tubs... parents did that while they were waiting for the little kids... nobody told them off."

"People vandalise the school because they're jealous. It makes us annoyed and angry and upset, it makes the place look so awful from the outside. They do it out of spite and don't think of the cost of repairs and who's got to find the money. They do it to hurt us because they know we like playing there and if they spoil it they are spoiling us."

4 Children's attitude and behaviour are influenced by the way the school grounds are managed

What is the purpose and value of the Informal Curriculum?

What happens now? How does the quality of the Informal Curriculum match your aims and objectives?

Do your Dinner Time Supervisors have a contract of employment and job description; how does this 'match' the role in reality?

How is current management practice and policy influencing children's attitude and behaviour?

Is the maintenance of the grounds affecting children's attitudes and behaviour?

SUGGESTED ACTIVITIES

Produce a statement defining your aims and objectives for the Informal Curriculum, i.e. why it exists and how it contributes to children's education and development. It may be necessary to explore this issue in some detail, ideally with the whole school community, in order to reach concensus.

Conduct structured observation sessions of playtime to establish exactly what children do, where and with whom. This could be undertaken by older pupils. Consult your schools council, if there is one. If not, find another way of consulting children. Consider a project on play: investigate the history of play; how parents and grandparents played; play and games from different cultures etc. as a way of exploring the subject.

Review the job description of DTSs with them. How does this mirror the aims and objectives you set for the Informal Curriculum. What particular problems do your DTSs experience? How might these be overcome or reduced?

Conduct a management analysis exercise to identify all the rules currently in force relating to use of the grounds. Brainstorm possible alternatives. If both pupils and staff are involved this exercise may not only produce some new and creative solutions, but will enhance relationships and extend everyone's understanding of the issues related to the management of the grounds.

Consider a 'Care for the Grounds Code' drawn up with the children to identify the problems and causes, and enlist their help in keeping the grounds in good condition. Include, for example, a litter policy and a procedure for reporting evidence of wear and tear or damage.

References from section three, chapter four

(1)   Sutton-Smith, B. ◆ 'School Playground as Festival' ◆ In *CEQ Vol.7 No.2* ◆ 1990 ◆ Children's Environments Research Group, The City University of New York.

(2)   Eifermann, Rivka ◆ 'It's child's play' ◆ In *Play: Its Role in Development and Evolution* ◆ Bruner, Jolly and Silva (Eds) ◆ 1976 ◆ Penguin.

(3)   Evans, John ◆ 'The teacher's role in playground supervision' ◆ In *Play and Culture Vol.3 No.3* (Journal of the Association for the Study of Play) ◆ August 1990 ◆ Human Kinetics.

(4)   Van der Kooij, Rimmert ◆ 'Play and Behavioural Disorders in Schoolchildren' ◆ In *Play and Culture* (Journal of the Association for the Study of Play) ◆ Human Kinetics.

(5)   O'Rourke, Maris ◆ 'In the Playground ◆ In *NZCER* (New Zealand Journal of Early Childhood Education).

(6)   Alstrom, B.B. ◆ *The School Yard* ◆ 1980 ◆ The Swedish Child Council.

(7)   Blatchford, Peter ◆ *Playtime in the Primary School: Problems and Improvements* ◆ 1989 ◆ NFER-NELSON ◆ ISBN 0 7005 1238 1.

(8)   Bjorklid, Pia ◆ *Schoolchildren and Joint Influence: Participation or Pseudo-democracy?* ◆ 1986 ◆ Stockholm Institute of Education.

(9)   Anon ◆ *Vandalism in schools and colleges, some possible ways of reducing damage* ◆ 1978 ◆ Department of Education and Science.

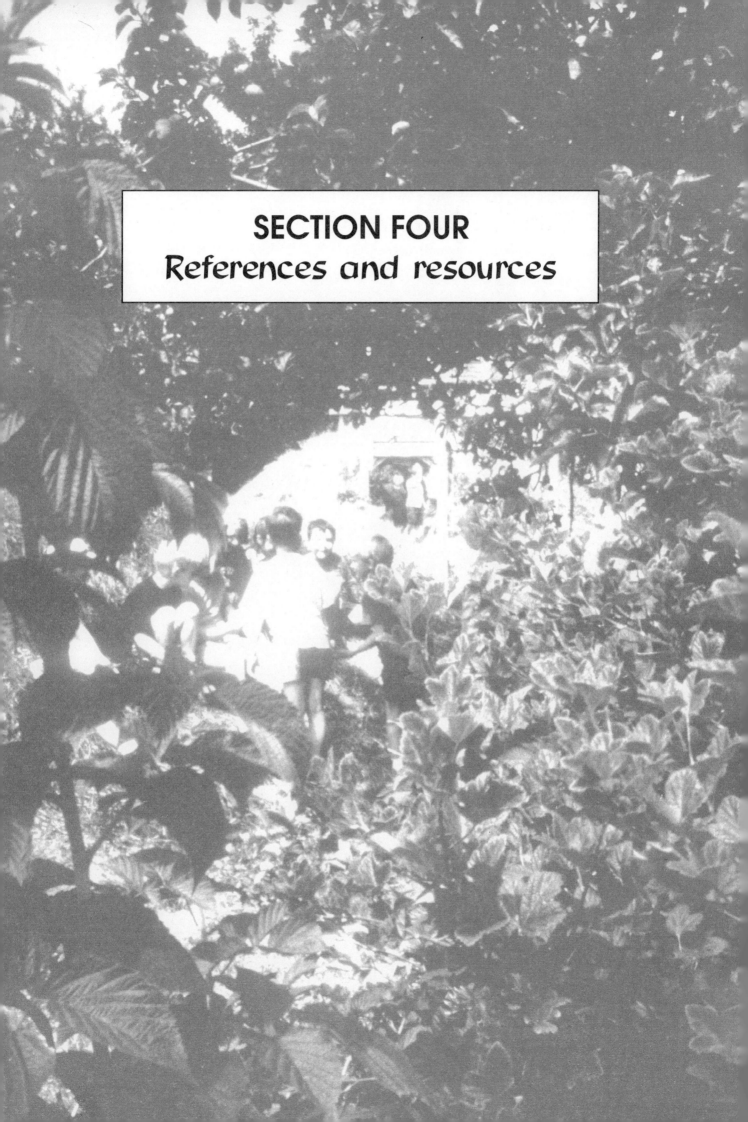

SECTION FOUR
References and resources

This Section contains:

◆ An alphabetical listing, by author, of references included throughout the document.

◆ Additional useful resource material.

1 Alphabetical listing of references (by author)

Aaron, D. and Winawer, B. ◆ *Child's Play: A Creative Approach to Playscapes for Today's Children* ◆ 1965 ◆ Harper & Row.

Adams, E. ◆ *Learning through Landscapes: The Final Report* ◆ 1990 ◆ ISBN 1 872865 01 1.

Adams, Eileen ◆ 'Back to Basics: Aesthetic Experience' ◆ In *CEQ Vol.8 No.2 Children's Aesthetic Experience of the Environment* ◆ 1991 ◆ ISSN 0886 0505.

Allen of Hurtwood, Lady Marjorie ◆ *Planning for Play* ◆ 1986 Thames and Hudson ◆ ISBN 0 500 270546 6.

Alstrom, B.B. ◆ *The School Yard* ◆ 1980 ◆ The Swedish Child Council.

Anon ◆ *Ask the Kids* ◆ 1975 ◆ Planning the School Site Research Project ◆ ISBN 0 900313 55 2.

Anon ◆ *The School Site Planning Handbook* ◆ 1977 ◆ Planning the School Site Research Project, Manchester Polytechnic.

Anon ◆ *Children's Exercise, Health and Fitness Fact Sheet* ◆ March 1988 ◆ The Sports Council.

Anon ◆ *Children's Range Behaviour* ◆ 1987 ◆ Play Board ◆ ISBN 0 948105 12 7.

Anon ◆ 'Discipline in Schools' - Report of the Comittee of Enquiry chaired by Lord Elton ◆ 1989 ◆ HMSO ◆ ISBN 0 11 270665 7.

Anon ◆ *Playtime: What really happens!* ◆ 1984 ◆ BBC Schools Radio.

Anon ◆ 'Pupils' Working Environment at School in Use' (EMILIA) ◆ In *School Research Newsletter* ◆ September 1985 ◆ Swedish National Board of Education.

Anon ◆ *Vandalism in schools and colleges, some possible ways of reducing damage* ◆ 1978 ◆ Department of Education and Science.

Anon ◆ *Young Eyes: Children's Vision of the Future Environment* ◆ 1990 ◆ The Henley Centre for Forecasting.

Berman, Ed. ◆ In *It's Child's Play Vol.1 No.4* ◆ November 1973 ◆ The Children and Youth Action Group Trust

Bishop, R.L., Peterson, G.L., Michaels, R.M. ◆ 'Measurement of children's preferences for the play environment' ◆ In *Environmental Design, Research and Practice* ◆ Mitchell, W.J. (Ed) ◆ 1972 ◆ Dowden, Hutchinson & Ross.

Bjorklid, Pia ◆ *Schoolchildren and Joint Influence: Participation or Pseudo-democracy?* ◆ 1986 ◆ Stockholm Institute of Education.

Blatchford, Peter ◆ *Playtime in the Primary School: Problems and Improvements* ◆ 1989 ◆ NFER-NELSON ◆ ISBN 0 7005 1238 1.

Boyce, E.R. ◆ *Infant School Activities* ◆ 1939 ◆ The Aberdeen University Press.

Brown, M. ◆ *Child Life in our Schools* ◆ 1906 ◆ George Philip & Son Ltd.

Bruce, T. ◆ *Time to Play in Early Childhood Education* ◆ 1991 ◆ Hodder & Stoughton ◆ ISBN 0 340 53878 3.

Carpenter, C.J., Huston, A., Spera, L. ◆ 'Children's Use of Time in Their Everyday Activities During Middle Childhood' ◆ In *The Ecological Context of Children's Play* ◆ Bloch and Pellegrini (Eds) ◆ Abley Publishing Corporation.

Chawla, Louise ◆ 'The Ecology of Environmental Memory' ◆ In *CEQ Vol.3 No.4* ◆ 1986 ◆ Children's Environments Research Group.

Christie, J. and Johnsen, E.P. ◆ 'The Constraints of Settings on Children's Play' ◆ In *Play and Culture Vol.2 No.4* ◆ November 1989.

Cobb, E. ◆ *The Ecology of Memory in Childhood* ◆ 1977 ◆ Columbia University Press.

David, Thomas G. ◆ 'Environmental Literacy' ◆ In *School Review* ◆ August 1974 ◆ University of Chicago Press.

Eifermann, Rivka ◆ 'It's child's play' ◆ In *Play: Its Role in Development and Evolution* ◆ Bruner, Jolly and Silva (Eds) ◆ 1976 ◆ Penguin.

Evans, John ◆ 'The teacher's role in playground supervision' ◆ In *Play and Culture Vol.3 No.3* ◆ August 1990.

Gibson, J.J. ◆ *The Eclogical Approach to Visual Perception* ◆ 1966 ◆ Houghton Mifflin.

Gump, P.V. ◆ 'Ecological Psychology and Issues of Play' ◆ In *The Ecological Context of Children's Play* ◆ Bloch and Pellegrini (Eds) ◆ Abley Publishing Corporation.

Hart, R. ◆ 'Children's Participation in Planning and Design: Theory, Research and Practice' ◆ In *Spaces for Children* ◆ Weinstein and David (Eds) ◆ 1987 ◆ Plenum Press ◆ ISBN 0 306 42423 1.

Hart, Roger ◆ *Children's Experience of Place* ◆ 1979 ◆ Irvington Publishers Inc. ◆ ISBN 0 470 99190 9.

Hart, Roger ◆ *Children's Participation: From Tokenism to Citizenship - Innocenti Essays No.4* ◆ UNICEF ◆ 1992 ◆ ISBN 88 85401 05 8.

Hillman, M., Adams. J., Whitelegg, J. ◆ *One False Move... A Study of Children's Independent Mobility* ◆ 1990 ◆ The Policy Studies Institute ◆ ISBN 0 85374 494 7.

Kerns, A. ◆ 'The Story of A Playground: Study of St. Mary's School, Erskinville' ◆ In *Architecture Australia No.68.*

Kirkby, MaryAnn ◆ 'Nature as refuge in children's environments' ◆ In *CEQ Vol.6 No.1 Children and Vegetation* ◆ Spring 1989 ◆ Children's Environments Research Group, The City University of New York ◆ ISSN 0886 0505.

King, Nancy R. ◆ 'Play: The Kindergartners' Perspective' ◆ In *The Elementary School Journal Vol.80 No.2* ◆ November 1979 ◆ The University of Chicago.

Little, Brian R. ◆ 'The social ecology of children's nothings' ◆ In *EKISTICS Vol.47 No.281* ◆ March/April 1980 ◆ Athens Center of Ekistics, Athens Technical Organisation, Greece ◆ ISSN 0013 2942.

Lukashok, A. and Lynch, K. ◆ 'Some childhood memories of the city' ◆ In *Journal of the American Institute of Planners* ◆ 1956.

Matthews, M. H. ◆ *Making Sense of Place - Children's Understanding of Large-Scale Environments* ◆ 1992 ◆ Harvester Wheatsheaf, Campus 400, Maryland Avenue, Hemel Hempstead, Herts HP2 7EZ ◆ 0 389 20987 2.

Moore, Robin ◆ 'Before and After Asphalt: Diversity as an Ecological Measure of Quality in Children's Outdoor Environments' ◆ In *The Ecological Context of Children's Play* ◆ Bloch and Pellegrini (Eds) ◆ Abley Publishing Corporation.

Moore, Robin ◆ *Childhood's Domain - Play and Place in Child Development* ◆ 1986 ◆ Croom Helm Ltd. ◆ ISBN 0 86664 939 8.

Moore, Robin ◆ 'Collaborating with young people to assess their landscape values' ◆ In *EKISTICS Vol.47 No.281* ◆ March/April 1980 ◆ Athens Center of Ekistics, Athens Technical Organisation, Greece ◆ ISSN 0013 2942.

Moore, Robin ◆ 'Generating Relevant Urban Childhood Places: Learning from the Yard' ◆ In *Innovations in Play Environments* ◆ Wilkinson, P. (Ed) ◆ 1980 ◆ Croom Helm Ltd. ◆ ISBN 0 7099 0024 4.

Noren-Bjorn, Eva ◆ *The Impossible Playground* ◆ 1982 ◆ Leisure Press ◆ ISBN 0 918438 88 8.

Olds, Anita ◆ 'Designing Settings for Infants and Toddlers' ◆ In *Spaces for Children* ◆ Weinstein and David (Eds) ◆ 1987 ◆ Plenum Press ◆ ISBN 0 306 42423 1.   155. 4

Olds, Anita ◆ 'Nature as Healer' ◆ In *CEQ Vol.6 No.1 Children and Vegetation* ◆ Spring 1989 ◆ Children's Environments Research Group, The City University of New York ◆ ISSN 0886 0505.

Opie, Iona and Peter ◆ *The Lore and Language of Schoolchildren* 1959 ◆ Oxford University Press ◆ ISBN 0 19 282059 1.

O'Rourke, Maris ◆ 'In the Playground' ◆ In *NZCER* (New Zealand Journal of Early Childhood Education).

Parkinson, C. ◆ *Children's Range Behaviour* ◆ 1987 ◆ Play Board ◆ ISBN 0 948105 12 7.

Proshansky, E. and Wolfe, M. ◆ 'The physical setting and open education' ◆ In *School Review* ◆ 1974.

Proshansky, H. and Fabian, A. ◆ 'The Development of Place Identity in the Child' ◆ In *Spaces for Children* ◆ Weinstein and David (Eds) ◆ 1987 ◆ Plenum Press ◆ ISBN 0 306 42423 1.

Relph, E. ◆ *Place and Placelessness* ◆ 1976 ◆ Pion Press, London.

Roberts, Alisdair ◆ *Out to Play: The Middle Years of Childhood* ◆ 1980 ◆ Aberdeen University Press ◆ ISBN 0 0802571 18 6.

Rothenberg, M., Hayward, D.G., Beasley, R. ◆ 'Playgrounds: For Whom?' ◆ In *Man-Environment Interactions - Part 111*, EDRA, 5 ◆ Carson, D.H. (Ed) ◆ 1974 ◆ Dowden, Hutchinson & Ross.

Saegert, S. and Hart, R. ◆ 'The development of environmental competence in boys and girls' ◆ In *Play: Anthropological perspectives* ◆ Salter, M. (Ed) ◆ 1978 ◆ Leisure Press, New York.

Schactel, E. ◆ 'On Memory and Childhood Amnesia' ◆ In *Journal of Biology and Pathology of Interpersonal Relations Vol.10* ◆ 1947.

Schneekloth, L.H. ◆ 'Where did you go? The Forest. What did you see? Nothing.' ◆ In *CEQ Vol.6 No.1 Children and Vegetation* ◆ Spring 1989 ◆ Children's Environments Research Group ◆ ISSN 0886 0505.

Shaw, Leland G. ◆ 'Designing playgrounds for able and disabled children' ◆ In *Spaces for Children* ◆ Weinstein and David (Eds) ◆ 1987 ◆ Plenum Press ◆ ISBN 0 306 42423 1.

Sleap, M. and Warburton, P. ◆ *Physical Activity Patterns of Primary School Children* ◆ 1990 ◆ The Happy Heart Project, Hull University.

Sutton-Smith, B. ◆ 'School Playground as Festival' ◆ In *CEQ Vol.7 No.2* ◆ 1990 ◆ Children's Environments Research Group, The City University of New York.

Tuan, Y.F. ◆ 'Children and the Natural Environment' ◆ In *Children and the Environment* ◆ Altman, I. and Wohlwill, J.F. (Eds) ◆ 1978 ◆ Plenum Press.

Van der Kooij, Rimmert ◆ 'Play and Behavioural Disorders in Schoolchildren' ◆ In *Play and Culture* (Journal of the Association for the Study of Play) ◆ Human Kinetics.

Vesin, Dr. P. ◆ 'Televised Violence and Young People' ◆ In *At Play* (Journal of PlayBoard Northern Ireland) *No.14.* ◆ June 1990.

Ward, Colin ◆ *The Child in the City* ◆ 1977 ◆ Architectural Press, London ◆ ISBN 0 85139 118 4.

Weinstein, C.S. and David, T.G. ◆ *Spaces for Children - The Built Environment and Child Development* ◆ 1987 ◆ Plenum Press ◆ ISBN 0 306 42423 1.

Zeisel, J. ◆ 'Designing out unintentional school property damage: A checklist' ◆ In *Man-Environment Interactions - Part 111*, EDRA 5 ◆ Carson, D.H. (Ed) ◆ 1974 ◆ Dowden, Hutchinson & Ross.

SCHOOLS GROUNDS DEVELOPMENT

Esso Schoolwatch, Learning through Landscapes, 3rd Floor, Southside Offices, The Law Courts, Winchester, SO23 9DL.
A two part package of materials designed to help schools improve their grounds. Includes 'The Initial Survey' for use by 8-18 year old pupils, and 'From Survey to Getting Started' containing practical activities to aid planning and development.

Play, Playtime and Playground, Wendy Titman, 1992, Learning through Landscapes/WWF UK, ISBN 1 872864 10 0, 17 pages.
A brief guide to key issues relating to play and playtime in primary schools. Designed to stimulate discussion amongst teachers, governors, supervisors and parents. Three copies are provided, as a pack, to enable wide circulation.

Can I stay in today Miss? - Improving the School Playground, Carol Ross and Amanda Ryan, 1990, Trentham Books, 151 Eturia Road, Stoke-on-Trent, Staffordshire, ST1 5NS, ISBN 0 948080 42 6, 80 pages.
Based on work undertaken with schools in Islington, this books offers practical strategies to improve the design of the physical environment and the management of playtime in order to enhance children's experience and behaviour.

PLAY THEORY

Play Behaviour, Joseph Levy, 1978, Robert E. Krieger Publishing Company Inc, Krieger Drive, Malabar, Fla 32950, ISBN 0 89874 627 2.
Provides a thorough analysis of play theories together with innovative approaches developed by the author which expand and extend the meaning and significance of play.

Time to Play in Early Childhood Education, Tina Bruce, 1991, Hodder & Stoughton, ISBN 0 340 53878-3, 178 pages.
Despite its title this book is a useful and interesting work for those involved with children of any age.

155.418

CHILDREN AND THE ENVIRONMENT

Alternative Learning Environments, Ed. Gary J Coates, Dowden, Hutchinson & Ross, Inc., 1974, ISBN 0 87933-037-6.
A collection of almost thirty papers by leading experts drawn from the fields of architecture, planning, education, psychology and landscape architecture. An inspiring, thought provoking and exciting work.

Greenprints for Changing Schools, Sue Greig, Graham Pike and David Selby, 1989, WWF/Kogan Page Ltd, ISBN 0 947613 08 0.
A challenging book which links the theory and practice of educational change.

Children's Environments, Children's Environments Research Group, E. & F. N. Spon, 2-6 Bounday Row, London, SE1 8HN.
This international journal features articles drawn from a wide range of disciplines dealing with theory, research, policy and applications relating to children from birth to 18 years.

CHILDREN'S GAMES

The Co-operative Sports and Games Book - Challenge without Competition, Terry Orlick, 1978, Pantheon Books, New York, ISBN 0 394 73494 7.
An invaluable book, not only because it is full of games ideas and practical strategies but because Terry Orlick expounds the basis and value of co-operative games so engagingly.

Games, Games, Games - A Co-operative Games Book, 1989, The Woodcraft Folk, 13 Ritherden Road, London, SW17 8QE.
Apart from containing details of several hundred games, the clarity and layout of this book makes it particularly useful.

Happy Heart's Playground Games Pack, 1992, Thomas Nelson & Sons Ltd, Nelson House, Mayfield Road, Walton-on-Thames, Surrey KT12 5PL, ISBN 0 17 423140 4.
A pack of thirty four laminated cards, giving clear instructions for games which require little or no equipment. Designed by the Happy Heart Project team to encourage increased physical

activity and fitness amongst children. The cards are suitable for use both indoors and in the playground with primary age children.

LUNCHTIME SUPERVISION AND MANAGEMENT

Guidelines for Primary Midday Supervisors, Jenny Mosley, 8 Westbourne Gardens, Trowbridge, Wilts BA14 0AJ.
Originally developed for Wiltshire Education Authority, this 15 page booklet includes simple and straightforward advice for mid-day supervisors, details of basic games and suggests strategies which schools can employ to help supervisors be happier in their work! Jenny Mosely produces a range of very useful material dealing with behaviour and discipline.

Lunchtime Supervision - The OPTIS guide to supervising in the lunch hour, 1986, OPTIS, OPTIS House, Cricket Road, Oxford OX4 3DW, ISBN 0 948 396 70 9.
An extremely comprehensive and well designed manual which covers all aspects of the role of lunchtime supervisors. By presenting 'situations' and examples of problems and difficulties encountered it provides an excellent active learning resource for training supervisors, both individually and in groups.

Playground Safety Guidelines, 1992, HMSO, ISBN 0 855 22405 3.
Prepared by the National Children's Play and Recreation Unit for the DES and the Welsh Office, this booklet provides advice on a range of safety issues. Available from National Play Information Centre, 359-361 Euston Road, London NW1 3AL.